The Algorithm Dictatorship

When Code Controls Civilization

Table of Contents

Introduction

In every era of human history, power has taken a recognizable form. Kingdoms were ruled by monarchs, nations governed by institutions, and economies shaped by industrial forces. Authority had a face, a voice, and often a visible structure that people could identify, question, or resist. Today, however, a new form of power has emerged—one that is neither elected nor easily seen, yet profoundly influential. It operates silently in the background of our daily lives, embedded in the systems we rely on, shaping decisions we believe to be our own. This is the rise of the invisible regime: algorithmic order.

Algorithms, once simple sets of instructions designed to solve specific problems, have evolved into complex, adaptive systems capable of learning, predicting, and influencing human behavior. They determine what we see, what we buy, what we believe, and even how we think. From the moment we wake up and check our phones to the time we fall asleep after scrolling through curated feeds, algorithms are continuously at work—filtering information, prioritizing content, and subtly guiding our actions. Unlike traditional systems of control, this new regime does not impose its authority through force or explicit command. Instead, it operates through optimization, personalization, and convenience.

The power of algorithms lies in their invisibility. They do not announce their presence or declare their intentions. They function quietly, embedded within platforms and technologies that have become essential to modern life. Social media feeds, search engines, navigation systems, online marketplaces, and even financial institutions are all governed by algorithmic logic. These systems analyze vast amounts of data—our preferences, behaviors, interactions—and use that information to predict and influence future actions. In doing so, they create a feedback loop where human behavior is both the input and the output of machine-driven processes.

This transformation represents a fundamental shift in how power is exercised. In the past, control was often centralized and overt. Today, it is distributed and covert, embedded in code rather than enforced by law alone. Decisions that were once made by humans—editors, managers, policymakers—are increasingly delegated to algorithms. These systems decide which news stories gain visibility, which job applications are shortlisted, which loans are approved, and which voices are amplified or silenced. The criteria behind these decisions are often opaque, hidden within complex models that even their creators may not fully understand.

At the heart of this new regime is data—the raw material that fuels algorithmic systems. Every click, search, and interaction generates data points that are collected, analyzed, and monetized. This data is not merely descriptive; it is predictive. It allows systems to anticipate our needs, desires, and vulnerabilities with remarkable accuracy. In this environment, human attention becomes a valuable commodity, and influencing behavior becomes a primary objective. Platforms are designed not just to serve users, but to engage and retain them, often by exploiting psychological triggers and cognitive biases.

Yet, the most striking aspect of this transformation is not the technology itself, but the subtlety of its influence. People rarely perceive themselves as being controlled by algorithms. On the contrary, the experience is often framed as empowerment—personalized recommendations, tailored content, and seamless user experiences. The illusion of choice remains intact, even as the range of options is carefully curated. This creates a paradox: individuals feel more autonomous than ever, while their decisions are increasingly shaped by unseen forces.

The implications of this shift extend far beyond individual behavior. Algorithmic systems are now deeply embedded in political, economic, and social structures. They influence public opinion, shape market dynamics, and redefine the boundaries of privacy and freedom. As these systems grow more sophisticated, the line between human agency and machine influence becomes increasingly blurred. The question is no longer whether algorithms affect our lives, but to what extent do they define them.

This book explores the rise of the algorithmic dictatorship system of control that operates not through coercion, but through code. It examines how algorithms have become the architects of modern civilization, shaping everything from personal choices to global systems. More importantly, it seeks to uncover the mechanisms behind this invisible regime and to question the assumptions that allow it to thrive.

Understanding this new form of power is the first step toward navigating it. In a world where code governs behavior and data drives decisions, awareness becomes a form of resistance. The invisible regime may not have a face, but its influence is undeniable. The challenge before us is to recognize it, understand it, and ultimately decide how much control we are willing to surrender in exchange for convenience.

Chapter 1

The Birth of the Algorithmic Age

The story of the algorithmic age does not begin with artificial intelligence, social media, or even computers. Its origins lie much deeper—in humanity's enduring quest to impose logic, order, and predictability on an uncertain world. Long before machines could process data, humans were already developing systematic methods to solve problems, optimize decisions, and understand patterns. These early logical frameworks, though simple by today's standards, laid the intellectual foundation for what would eventually become algorithms.

An algorithm, at its core, is nothing more than a defined set of instructions designed to achieve a specific outcome. Ancient mathematicians used algorithmic thinking to perform calculations, solve equations, and organize knowledge. Over time, this structured approach to problem-solving evolved, becoming increasingly formalized and abstract. What began as manual processes carried out by human minds gradually transitioned into automated systems capable of executing these instructions with speed and precision far beyond human capability.

The true turning point came with the advent of computing. The development of early computers transformed algorithms from theoretical constructs into practical tools. Machines could now process vast amounts of information, execute repetitive tasks, and produce consistent results without fatigue or error. Initially, these systems were limited in scope—used primarily for scientific calculations, military applications, and industrial processes. Their purpose was clear, their function narrowly defined, and their influence relatively contained.

However, as computational power increased and digital technologies became more widespread, algorithms began to expand beyond their original roles. They were no longer confined to solving isolated problems; they started to shape entire systems. The rise of the internet marked a critical phase in this transformation. For the first time, algorithms were deployed at a global scale, managing the flow of information across interconnected networks. Search engines emerged, using algorithms to index and rank vast amounts of content, determining what information was accessible and visible to users.

This shift introduced a new dimension of influence. Algorithms were no longer just tools for calculation—they became gatekeepers of knowledge. The information people encountered was no longer random or purely user-driven; it was curated, filtered, and prioritized by algorithmic systems. This marked the beginning of a subtle but profound change in how individuals interacted with information and, consequently, how they understood the world.

As digital platforms evolved, so did the sophistication of algorithms. The introduction of machine learning allowed systems to move beyond static instructions and adapt based on data. Instead of being explicitly programmed for every scenario, algorithms could now learn from patterns, refine their outputs, and improve over time. This capability unlocked unprecedented potential, enabling systems to perform tasks such as image recognition, language processing, and predictive analytics with remarkable accuracy.

At the same time, the volume of data being generated began to grow exponentially. Every interaction—every click, search, purchase, and movement—produced data that could be collected and analyzed. This data became the fuel that powered algorithmic systems, allowing them to make increasingly precise predictions about human behavior. The relationship between humans and algorithms entered a new phase: one where machines were not just responding to human input but actively anticipating it.

This evolution gave rise to a new paradigm—one in which algorithms became deeply embedded in the infrastructure of modern life. They began to influence decisions in areas as diverse as finance, healthcare, transportation, and entertainment. Recommendation systems suggested what to watch, buy, or read. Navigation algorithms determined the fastest routes. Financial models assessed creditworthiness. In each case, algorithms were making decisions that directly impacted human experiences and outcomes.

Yet, as their influence grew, so did their complexity. Modern algorithms, particularly those based on advanced machine learning techniques, often operate as "black boxes." Their internal processes are not easily understood, even by experts. This opacity introduces a critical challenge: decisions that affect millions of people are being made by systems whose logic is not fully transparent or accountable.

The birth of the algorithmic age, therefore, is not simply a technological milestone—it is a transformation in how power operates within society. Algorithms have moved from the periphery to the center, from tools to decision-makers, from assistants to architects of systems. They shape not only what we do, but how systems function and evolve.

Understanding this origin is essential. To grasp the full implications of the algorithmic dictatorship, one must first recognize how these systems emerged, how they evolved, and how they became so deeply integrated into the fabric of modern civilization. The algorithmic age was not created overnight; it is the result of decades of innovation, driven by a desire for efficiency, accuracy, and control.

What began as a method for solving problems has become a force that defines them.

From Mechanical Logic to Machine Intelligence

The journey from mechanical logic to machine intelligence represents one of the most profound transformations in human history. It is a progression not only of technology, but of thought itself, an evolution in how humanity conceptualizes problem-solving, decision-making, and ultimately, intelligence. What began as simple, rule-based systems has matured into complex, adaptive networks capable of learning, predicting, and, in many ways, mimicking aspects of human cognition. To understand the present algorithmic landscape, it is essential to trace this journey from its mechanical origins to its intelligent present.

Mechanical logic, in its earliest form, was rooted in the desire to standardize reasoning. Long before the digital age, humans sought ways to formalize thought processes into repeatable steps. This impulse can be seen in early mathematical procedures, where problems were solved through clearly defined sequences. However, the real shift occurred when these logical steps were embedded into physical systems. Mechanical devices—such as early calculators and analytical engines—were designed to execute predefined instructions automatically. These machines did not "think" in any meaningful sense; they followed rules with precision and consistency. Their intelligence, if it could be called that, was entirely derived from the logic imposed upon them by their creators.

One of the defining characteristics of mechanical logic was determinism. Every input produced a predictable output, governed by a fixed set of rules. There was no ambiguity, no adaptation, and no capacity for learning. This made mechanical systems reliable but limited. They excelled at repetitive, structured tasks but struggled with complexity, uncertainty, and variability—elements that are inherent to real-world environments. Nevertheless, these early systems established a critical principle: that reasoning could be externalized, encoded, and executed independently of the human mind.

The transition from mechanical logic to digital computation marked the next major phase in this evolution. With the advent of electronic computers, logic was no longer constrained by physical gears and levers. Instead, it was represented through binary code—streams of zeros and ones that could be processed at unprecedented speeds. This shift allowed for far greater flexibility and scalability. Programs could be written, modified, and executed with relative ease, enabling machines to handle increasingly complex tasks.

Despite this advancement, early digital systems remained fundamentally rule-based. Programmers had to anticipate every possible scenario and explicitly define how the machine should respond. This approach, while effective in controlled environments, revealed its limitations as problems grew more complex. Real-world situations often involve incomplete information, uncertainty, and dynamic conditions that cannot be fully captured by static rules. It became clear that a new paradigm was needed—one that allowed machines to move beyond rigid instruction sets.

This need gave rise to the concept of machine intelligence. Unlike mechanical logic, which relies on predefined rules, machine intelligence is characterized by adaptability. Instead of being told exactly what to do, machines are designed to learn from data, identify patterns, and make decisions based on experience. This shift represents a fundamental departure from traditional computing. The focus is no longer on programming explicit instructions, but on creating systems that can generate their own rules through learning processes.

At the heart of this transformation is the field of machine learning. Machine learning algorithms are designed to analyze data, detect patterns, and improve their performance over time. They operate by adjusting internal parameters in response to feedback, effectively "learning" from experience. This allows them to handle tasks that would be impractical or impossible to solve through traditional programming methods. For example, recognizing faces in images, understanding natural language, or predicting consumer behavior all require the ability to process vast amounts of data and adapt to new information.

A key driver of machine intelligence has been the exponential growth of data. In the digital age, data is generated at an unprecedented scale, providing the raw material that machine learning systems require. Every interaction, whether it is a search query, a social media post, or a financial transaction—contributes to a growing pool of information that can be analyzed and leveraged. This abundance of data enables machines to identify subtle patterns and correlations that would be difficult for humans to detect.

Another critical factor is the advancement of computational power. Modern processors, combined with specialized hardware such as graphics processing units (GPUs), allow for the rapid processing of large datasets and complex models. This computational capability has made it possible to train sophisticated machine learning systems, including deep neural networks, which are inspired by the structure of the human brain. These networks consist of multiple layers of interconnected nodes, each processing information and passing it to the next layer. Through this layered approach, neural networks can extract increasingly abstract features from data, enabling them to perform tasks such as image recognition and language translation with remarkable accuracy.

Despite their capabilities, machine intelligence systems differ fundamentally from human intelligence. They do not possess consciousness, self-awareness, or genuine understanding. Their "intelligence" is statistical rather than conceptual; they identify patterns and make predictions based on probabilities, not meaning. This distinction is crucial, as it highlights both the power and the limitations of machine intelligence. While these systems can outperform humans in specific tasks, they lack the broader contextual awareness and reasoning abilities that characterize human cognition.

Nevertheless, the impact of machine intelligence on society is profound. As these systems become more integrated into various aspects of life, they begin to influence decision-making processes at multiple levels. In business, machine learning models are used to optimize operations, forecast demand, and personalize customer experiences. In healthcare, they assist in diagnosing diseases and recommending treatments. In finance, they analyze market trends and manage risk. In each case, machine intelligence enhances efficiency and accuracy, but also introduces new challenges related to transparency, accountability, and control.

One of the most significant implications of this transition is the shift in how decisions are made. In traditional systems, decisions are based on human judgment, informed by experience and reasoning. In algorithmic systems, decisions are increasingly delegated to machines that operate based on data-driven models. This can lead to more consistent and objective outcomes, but it also raises concerns about bias and fairness. Machine learning systems are only as good as the data they are trained on, and if that data reflects existing inequalities or biases, the resulting models may perpetuate or even amplify those issues.

Furthermore, the complexity of modern machine intelligence systems often makes them difficult to interpret. Unlike mechanical logic, where the reasoning process is explicit and traceable, machine learning models—particularly deep neural networks—can be opaque. This lack of transparency creates a "black box" problem, where it is challenging to understand how decisions are being made. This poses significant risks in high-stakes applications, such as healthcare or criminal justice, where accountability is essential.

As we move further into the algorithmic age, the distinction between mechanical logic and machine intelligence continues to blur. Many systems combine elements of both, using rule-based frameworks alongside adaptive learning components. This hybrid approach allows for greater flexibility and control but also increases complexity. The challenge lies in managing this complexity while ensuring that these systems remain aligned with human values and societal goals.

The journey from mechanical logic to machine intelligence is not merely technological progression; it is a shift in the locus of control. Where once humans defined every rule and decision, machines are now capable of generating and refining their own. This does not mean that humans are no longer in control, but it does mean that control is becoming more distributed and less direct. Understanding this shift is essential for navigating the future, as it raises fundamental questions about autonomy, responsibility, and the role of technology in shaping human life.

In essence, the evolution from mechanical logic to machine intelligence marks the transition from systems that execute instructions to systems that interpret, adapt, and influence. It is the foundation upon which the algorithmic dictatorship is built—a world where code does not merely follow orders but increasingly determines them.

The Evolution of Data-Driven Systems

The evolution of data-driven systems represents a defining trajectory in the development of modern technology and society. It marks the transition from intuition-based decision-making to a world increasingly governed by empirical evidence, statistical modeling, and predictive analytics. This transformation did not occur abruptly; rather, it unfolded through a series of incremental advancements, each expanding the role of data in shaping systems, institutions, and human behavior. Understanding this evolution is essential to grasp how data has become the central force powering the algorithmic age.

In its earliest form, data was scarce, fragmented, and difficult to process. Organizations relied heavily on human judgment, experience, and limited records to make decisions. Data collection was manual, often confined to physical documents, and analysis was constrained by the capabilities of human cognition. While statistics as a discipline provided tools for interpreting data, its application was limited by the availability and accessibility of information. Decisions were often reactive, based on historical trends rather than real-time insights.

The introduction of digital technologies fundamentally altered this landscape. With the advent of computers, data could be stored, organized, and processed more efficiently. Early database systems allowed organizations to manage structured information, such as customer records, inventory lists, and financial transactions. These systems marked the beginning of data-driven operations, enabling more informed decision-making based on quantifiable metrics. However, the scope of these systems remained relatively narrow, focusing primarily on internal processes and structured data formats.

As computing capabilities advanced, so did the complexity and scale of data systems. The emergence of relational databases in the late twentieth century introduced a more sophisticated approach to data management. Data could now be organized into interconnected tables, allowing for more flexible querying and analysis. This development facilitated the integration of data across different functions within organizations, providing a more comprehensive view of operations. Decision-making became increasingly data-informed, as managers could access detailed reports and analytics to guide their strategies.

The next major phase in the evolution of data-driven systems was characterized by the rise of the internet. The digitalization of communication and commerce generated an unprecedented volume of data, extending far beyond the boundaries of individual organizations. Every online interaction, whether browsing a website, sending an email, or making purchase-produced data that could be captured and analyzed. This shift marked the transition from structured, internally generated data to vast streams of unstructured, externally sourced information.

The concept of "big data" emerged in response to this explosion of information. Big data is not defined solely by its volume, but also by its velocity and variety. Data is generated continuously, in real time, and in diverse formats, including text, images, audio, and video. Traditional data processing methods proved inadequate for handling this scale and complexity, leading to the development of new technologies and frameworks designed to store and analyze large datasets. Distributed computing systems, such as those based on cloud infrastructure, enabled organizations to process data at scale, unlocking new possibilities for analysis and insight.

With the ability to process vast amounts of data came the opportunity to move beyond descriptive analytics toward predictive and prescriptive models. Descriptive analytics focuses on understanding what has happened in the past, while predictive analytics uses statistical techniques and machine learning algorithms to forecast future outcomes. Prescriptive analytics goes a step further, recommending actions based on these predictions. This progression represents a significant shift in the role of data—from a tool for understanding history to a mechanism for shaping the future.

Machine learning played a pivotal role in this transformation. Unlike traditional statistical models, which rely on predefined assumptions, machine learning algorithms can adapt to data, identifying patterns and relationships without explicit programming. This adaptability allows for more accurate predictions and more nuanced insights. For example, recommendation systems analyze user behavior to suggest products or content, while fraud detection systems identify anomalous patterns that may indicate suspicious activity. In each case, the system improves over time as it processes more data.

Another critical development in the evolution of data-driven systems is the integration of real-time analytics. In earlier stages, data analysis was often conducted in batches, with insights generated after a delay. Modern systems, however, can process data as it is generated, enabling immediate responses to changing conditions. This capability is particularly important in contexts such as financial trading, cybersecurity, and supply chain management, where timely decisions can have significant consequences. Real-time data processing transforms systems from reactive to proactive, allowing them to anticipate and respond to events as they unfold.

The proliferation of connected devices has further accelerated the growth of data-driven systems. The Internet of Things (IoT) encompasses a wide range of devices—from smartphones and wearable technology to industrial sensors and smart home appliances—that continuously collect and transmit data. These devices generate a constant stream of information about physical environments, user behavior, and system performance. This data can be used to optimize operations, enhance user experience, and enable new forms of automation. For instance, smart thermostats adjust temperature settings based on usage patterns, while industrial sensors monitor equipment to predict maintenance needs.

As data-driven systems have become more pervasive, their influence has extended beyond individual organizations to entire ecosystems. Platforms such as social media networks, e-commerce marketplaces, and search engines operate as data-driven ecosystems, where interactions between users generate data that feed back into the system. These platforms leverage data to optimize engagement, personalize experiences, and maximize revenue. The result is a self-reinforcing cycle in which data drives system behavior, and system behavior generates more data.

This evolution has also given rise to new economic models centered around data. Data is increasingly viewed as an asset, often referred to as the "new oil." Companies collect, analyze, and monetize data, using it to gain competitive advantages and drive innovation. This has led to the emergence of data-centric business models, where the primary value lies not in physical products, but in the insights derived from data. Advertising platforms, for example, use data to target specific audiences with precision, while streaming services use viewing data to inform content production and recommendations.

However, the rise of data-driven systems is not without challenges. One of the most significant concerns is the issue of privacy. As data collection becomes more extensive and granular, individuals may have limited awareness or control over how their data is used. This raises questions about consent, ownership, and the ethical use of information. Regulatory frameworks, such as data protection laws, have been introduced to address these concerns, but the rapid pace of technological change often outstrips the ability of regulation to keep up.

Another challenge is the potential for bias in data-driven systems. Data reflects the conditions under which it is generated, including existing social, economic, and cultural biases. When machine learning models are trained on biased data, they may produce biased outcomes, reinforcing or exacerbating inequalities. This issue highlights the importance of data quality, transparency, and accountability in the design and deployment of data-driven systems.

The increasing reliance on data also raises questions about human agency. As systems become more capable of making decisions based on data, there is a risk that human judgment may be marginalized. While data-driven decisions can enhance efficiency and objectivity, they may also reduce the role of human intuition, creativity, and ethical reasoning. Striking a balance between data-driven insights and human oversight is a critical challenge in the ongoing evolution of these systems.

In conclusion, the evolution of data-driven systems reflects a broader shift in how society operates and makes decisions. From the early days of manual data collection to the sophisticated, real-time analytics of today, data has become the foundation of modern systems. It drives innovation, shapes behavior, and influences outcomes at every level. As we continue to advance into the algorithmic age, the role of data will only become more central, raising both opportunities and challenges that must be carefully navigated.

The journey of data-driven systems is far from complete. It is an ongoing process, shaped by technological advancements, societal needs, and ethical considerations. Understanding this evolution provides a critical perspective on the forces that are shaping our world—and the systems that increasingly govern it.

The Emergence of Predictive Technologies

The emergence of predictive technologies marks a decisive shift in the trajectory of modern systems—from reacting to events after they occur to anticipating them before they unfold. This transition represents one of the most powerful and consequential developments in the algorithmic age. It redefines how decisions are made, how risks are managed, and how behavior is influenced. At its core, predictive technology is not merely about forecasting the future; it is about shaping it through data-driven insight.

Historically, human decision-making has been rooted in hindsight. Individuals and institutions relied on past experiences, historical records, and observable trends to guide their actions. While this approach provided a degree of stability, it was inherently limited. The future remained uncertain, and decisions were often reactive rather than proactive. The desire to reduce this uncertainty gave rise to statistical modeling, where probabilities were used to estimate future outcomes based on known variables. However, these early models were constrained by limited data and computational power, restricting their accuracy and applicability.

The foundation of predictive technologies lies in the convergence of three critical elements: data, algorithms, and computational capacity. As digital systems began to generate vast amounts of data, the raw material necessary for prediction became increasingly abundant. Every interaction, whether it is a purchase, a search query, a social media engagement, or a geographic movement—creates a data point that can be analyzed. Over time, these data points accumulate into large datasets that capture patterns of behavior, preferences, and trends.

Algorithms serve as the mechanisms through which this data is transformed into insight. In traditional systems, algorithms follow predefined rules to process information. Predictive technologies, however, rely on more advanced forms of computation, particularly machine learning. These systems are not explicitly programmed to predict specific outcomes; instead, they are trained on data to identify patterns and relationships. Through iterative processes, they refine their internal models, improving their predictive accuracy over time.

The third component—computational capacity—enables these processes to occur at scale. Modern computing infrastructure, including cloud platforms and specialized hardware, allows for the rapid processing of massive datasets and complex models. This capability is essential for predictive technologies, as it allows them to analyze data in real time and generate actionable insights with minimal delay.

One of the defining characteristics of predictive technologies is their reliance on patterns. Human behavior, while seemingly complex and unpredictable, often exhibits consistent patterns when observed at scale. These patterns can be subtle, emerging only when large volumes of data are analyzed. Predictive systems are designed to detect these patterns and use them to forecast future behavior. For example, by analyzing past purchasing behavior, a system can predict what products a consumer is likely to buy. Similarly, by examining user interactions on a platform, it can anticipate what content will capture attention.

This capability has transformed numerous industries. In the commercial sector, predictive technologies are used to personalize experiences, optimize operations, and increase efficiency. Recommendation systems suggest products, movies, or content based on user preferences. Supply chain systems forecast demand, enabling companies to manage inventory more effectively. Marketing strategies are tailored to target specific audiences with precision, maximizing engagement and conversion rates.

In healthcare, predictive technologies are used to improve diagnosis, treatment, and patient outcomes. By analyzing medical records, genetic data, and lifestyle information, systems can identify risk factors and predict the likelihood of diseases. This allows for earlier intervention and more personalized care. In finance, predictive models assess credit risk, detect fraudulent activity, and guide investment decisions. In each of these domains, the ability to anticipate future events provides a significant advantage.

However, the influence of predictive technologies extends beyond efficiency and optimization. It fundamentally alters the nature of decision-making. In traditional systems, decisions are made based on explicit reasoning and human judgment. In predictive systems, decisions are increasingly guided by probabilistic models. These models do not provide certainty; they offer likelihoods. A predictive system does not say what will happen, it estimates what is most likely to happen based on available data.

This probabilistic approach introduces both opportunities and challenges. On one hand, it allows for more informed decision-making, reducing uncertainty and improving outcomes. On the other hand, it raises questions about reliability and trust. Predictions are only as accurate as the data and models that generate them. If the underlying data is incomplete, biased, or unrepresentative, the predictions may be flawed. This can lead to incorrect decisions, with potentially significant consequences.

Another critical aspect of predictive technologies is their feedback loop. Predictions do not exist in isolation; they influence behavior, which in turn generates new data that feeds back into the system. For example, if a recommendation system suggests certain content, users are more likely to engage with it. This engagement reinforces the system's understanding of user preferences, leading to more similar recommendations in the future. Over time, this feedback loop can create self-reinforcing patterns, shaping behavior in ways that may not be immediately apparent.

This dynamic has profound implications for autonomy and control. Predictive technologies do not merely observe behavior; they can influence it. By anticipating what individuals are likely to do, systems can guide them toward specific actions. This influence is often subtle, embedded in the design of platforms and interfaces. Users may feel that they are making independent choices, while their options have been curated and prioritized by predictive models.

The ethical dimensions of predictive technologies are complex and multifaceted. One of the primary concerns is privacy. The effectiveness of predictive systems depends on access to large amounts of personal data. This raises questions about how data is collected, stored, and used. Individuals may not fully understand the extent to which their data is being analyzed or the purposes for which it is being used. Ensuring transparency and informed consent is a significant challenge in this context.

Bias is another critical issue. Predictive models are trained on historical data, which may reflect existing inequalities or prejudices. If these biases are not addressed, the models may perpetuate or amplify them. For example, in hiring or lending decisions, biased data can lead to discriminatory outcomes. Addressing this issue requires careful consideration of data quality, model design, and evaluation processes.

The opacity of predictive systems also presents challenges. Many advanced models, particularly those based on deep learning, operate as "black boxes," where the internal logic is not easily interpretable. This lack of transparency makes it difficult to understand how predictions are generated or to identify potential errors. In high-stakes applications, this can undermine accountability and trust.

Despite these challenges, the trajectory of predictive technologies continues to advance. Innovations in artificial intelligence, data processing, and computational infrastructure are expanding the capabilities of these systems. They are becoming more accurate, more efficient, and more integrated into everyday life. As this integration deepens, predictive technologies are likely to play an increasingly central role in shaping societal structures and individual experiences.

The emergence of predictive technologies represents a shift from a world that reacts to events to one that anticipates and, in many cases, influences them. It is a transformation that redefines the relationship between humans and machines, between data and decision-making, and between present actions and future outcomes. While these technologies offer significant benefits, they also introduce new complexities that must be carefully managed.

Ultimately, predictive technologies are not just tools, they are systems of influence. They shape what is seen, what is chosen, and what is possible. In doing so, they become a foundational element of the algorithmic dictatorship, where control is exercised not through direct command, but through the anticipation and guidance of behavior. Understanding their emergence is essential to understanding the broader forces that define the modern digital landscape.

When Software Became Infrastructure

For much of its early history, software was perceived as a tool—an auxiliary layer that supported physical systems, automated calculations, and facilitated discrete tasks. It existed alongside infrastructure, not as infrastructure itself. Roads, power grids, water systems, and telecommunications networks formed the backbone of societies, while software operated within these domains as a means of efficiency. Over time, however, this relationship fundamentally changed. Software did not merely support infrastructure; it became infrastructure. This transformation represents one of the most consequential shifts in the modern era, redefining how societies function, how economies operate, and how power is exercised.

The transition from software as a tool to software as infrastructure began with the increasing digitization of essential services. As industries adopted computer systems to manage operations, software moved from peripheral applications to central control mechanisms. Early examples can be seen in banking systems, where software began to manage transactions, account balances, and financial records. What was once handled manually became fully dependent on digital systems. Over time, this dependency deepened. The functioning of financial institutions became inseparable from the software that powered them.

A similar transformation occurred in telecommunications. Traditional communication systems relied on physical infrastructure such as cables and switches, but software gradually assumed control over routing, signal processing, and network management. The emergence of the internet accelerated this shift, introducing a new form of infrastructure that was inherently software-driven. Unlike physical networks, the internet operates through protocols—sets of rules encoded in software that govern how data is transmitted and received. These protocols form the invisible architecture of global communication, enabling billions of devices to connect and interact seamlessly.

As software systems expanded, they began to orchestrate increasingly complex operations. In transportation, software controls traffic systems, manages logistics, and optimizes routes. Airlines rely on software for scheduling, navigation, and safety systems. In energy sectors, software monitors and regulates power distribution, balancing supply and demand across grids. These systems are no longer optional enhancements; they are integral to the functioning of infrastructure. Without software, these networks would cease to operate effectively.

The rise of cloud computing marked a critical turning point in this evolution. Traditionally, software was installed and operated on individual machines or localized servers. Cloud computing abstracted this model, allowing software and data to be hosted on remote servers and accessed over the internet. This shift transformed software into a shared, scalable resource. Organizations no longer needed to maintain their own infrastructure; they could rely on cloud platforms to provide computing power, storage, and services on demand. In effect, the cloud became a new layer of infrastructure—one that is entirely software-defined.

This development introduced a new level of centralization. A relatively small number of technology companies began to control vast portions of the world's digital infrastructure. These entities provide the platforms upon which businesses, governments, and individuals operate. From data storage to application hosting, their systems underpin a wide range of activities. This concentration of control raises important questions about power, dependency, and resilience. When software becomes infrastructure, those who control the software wield significant influence over the systems that depend on it.

Another defining feature of software as infrastructure is its programmability. Unlike physical infrastructure, which is relatively static, software-based systems can be modified, updated, and reconfigured with relative ease. This flexibility allows for rapid adaptation to changing conditions. For example, software updates can enhance security, introduce new features, or fix vulnerabilities without requiring physical changes to infrastructure. This dynamic nature is a key advantage, enabling systems to evolve continuously.

However, this programmability also introduces new risks. Changes to software can have widespread and immediate effects, particularly when systems are interconnected. A single error or vulnerability can propagate across networks, disrupting services on a large scale. Cybersecurity becomes a critical concern, as malicious actors may exploit weaknesses in software to gain access to infrastructure. The reliance on software thus introduces a new dimension of vulnerability, where threats are not physical but digital.

The integration of software into infrastructure has also transformed the concept of access. In traditional systems, access to infrastructure was often determined by physical proximity or ownership. In software-driven systems, access is mediated by digital interfaces and controlled by code. Permissions, authentication, and authorization mechanisms determine who can use services and under what conditions. This creates a new form of gatekeeping, where access is governed by algorithms rather than physical constraints.

In urban environments, the concept of the "smart city" exemplifies the role of software as infrastructure. Sensors, connected devices, and data analytics systems are used to monitor and manage urban systems such as traffic, energy consumption, and public services. These systems rely on software to collect data, analyze patterns, and make decisions in real time. The city itself becomes a data-driven environment, where infrastructure is not only physical but also digital. This integration offers the potential for increased efficiency and sustainability, but it also raises concerns about surveillance, privacy, and control.

Economic systems have likewise been reshaped by software infrastructure. Digital platforms facilitate transactions, connect buyers and sellers, and manage supply chains. E-commerce, digital payments, and online services operate on software platforms that function as infrastructure for economic activity. These platforms create ecosystems where interactions are mediated by algorithms, influencing pricing, visibility, and competition. The boundaries between infrastructure and market become blurred, as platforms simultaneously provide the environment and participate within it.

The transformation of software into infrastructure also has profound implications for governance. Governments increasingly rely on software systems to deliver public services, manage data, and enforce regulations. Digital identity systems, tax collection platforms, and public health databases are all examples of software-based infrastructure. This reliance introduces new challenges related to transparency, accountability, and oversight. Decisions made by software systems may not be easily understood or scrutinized, raising questions about democratic control.

One of the most significant aspects of this transformation is the invisibility of software infrastructure. Unlike physical infrastructure, which is tangible and observable, software operates in the background. Users interact with interfaces, often unaware of the complex systems that underpin them. This invisibility can lead to a lack of awareness about the extent of dependency on software. It also makes it more difficult to identify and address issues when they arise.

The convergence of software and infrastructure represents a shift in the nature of control. In traditional systems, control was exercised through physical means—ownership of land, resources, or facilities. In software-driven systems, control is exercised through code. The rules that govern systems are embedded in software, and those who write and maintain this code have the ability to shape how systems operate. This introduces a new form of power, one that is less visible but highly influential.

As software continues to evolve, its role as infrastructure is likely to expand further. Emerging technologies such as artificial intelligence, blockchain, and edge computing are extending the capabilities of software systems, enabling new forms of interaction and coordination. These developments will further integrate software into the fabric of society, making it an even more critical component of infrastructure.

In conclusion, the moment when software became infrastructure marks a fundamental transformation in how systems are designed, managed, and experienced. Software is no longer a supporting element; it is the foundation upon which modern systems are built. It governs the flow of information, the operation of services, and the interactions between individuals and institutions. This transformation brings significant benefits in terms of efficiency, scalability, and adaptability, but it also introduces new challenges related to control, security, and accountability.

Understanding this shift is essential for navigating the algorithmic age. As software continues to underpin critical systems, its influence will only grow. Recognizing software as infrastructure is not merely a technical observation—it is a recognition of a new reality, where the foundations of society are increasingly defined by code.

Chapter 2

Data – The Currency of Control

In the architecture of the modern digital world, data has assumed a role far more powerful than its technical definition suggests. It is no longer merely a byproduct of activity or a passive record of events. Instead, data has become the foundational resource that fuels systems, drives decisions, and enables control. In this sense, data functions as a new form of currency—one that is intangible, continuously generated, and deeply embedded in the fabric of everyday life. Unlike traditional currencies, which are exchanged explicitly, data is often produced unconsciously, collected silently, and utilized in ways that extend far beyond the awareness of those who generate it.

The transformation of data into a form of currency did not occur overnight. It emerged gradually as digital technologies expanded and interconnected systems began to rely on information as their primary input. In earlier stages of technological development, data served a descriptive function. It recorded transactions, tracked inventory, and documented events. Its value was limited to its ability to provide insight into what had already occurred. However, as computational capabilities advanced and analytical techniques became more sophisticated, the role of data evolved. It shifted from describing the past to shaping the future.

At the core of this transformation is the realization that data is not just information—it is influence. When collected and analyzed at scale, data reveals patterns of behavior, preferences, and tendencies. These patterns can be used to predict actions, guide decisions, and ultimately shape outcomes. In this way, data becomes a mechanism of control. It allows systems to anticipate human behavior and respond in ways that align with specific objectives, whether commercial, political, or social.

The economic dimension of data further reinforces its status as a currency. In the digital economy, data is exchanged for services, often without explicit acknowledgment. Users access platforms, applications, and content in return for providing data about their behavior, interests, and interactions. This exchange is rarely perceived as a transaction, yet it forms the basis of many modern business models. Companies collect and analyze data to generate insights, which are then monetized through targeted advertising, personalized services, and strategic decision-making. The more data a system possesses, the greater its capacity to generate value.

This dynamic has led to the emergence of a data-driven economy, where the accumulation and control of data confer significant advantages. Organizations that can collect, process, and interpret large volumes of data are able to operate more efficiently, innovate more rapidly, and compete more effectively. As a result, data has become a strategic asset, often compared to natural resources such as oil. However, unlike physical resources, data is non-rivalrous—it can be replicated and used simultaneously by multiple entities. Its value lies not in its scarcity, but in its application.

The pervasive nature of data collection is a defining characteristic of this new landscape. Every digital interaction generates data, often in ways that are invisible to the user. Devices, platforms, and systems continuously capture information about location, behavior, preferences, and interactions. This process creates a comprehensive digital footprint, a detailed record of an individual's activities and tendencies. Over time, these footprints accumulate into extensive datasets that provide a granular view of human behavior.

This continuous flow of data enables the development of highly sophisticated systems capable of real-time analysis and decision-making. These systems do not merely respond to inputs; they actively interpret and act upon data as it is generated. This capability transforms data into a dynamic resource, one that is constantly updated and refined. The result is a feedback loop in which data informs decisions, decisions influence behavior, and behavior generates new data.

However, the framing of data as a currency also introduces critical questions about ownership and control. Unlike traditional currencies, which are typically owned and managed by individuals or institutions, data often exists in a more ambiguous state. Individuals generate data through their actions, but the systems that collect and store this data are controlled by organizations. This creates a complex relationship in which the producers of data may have limited control over how it is used. The question of who owns data—and who benefits from it—becomes central to understanding its role in modern systems.

The power of data is further amplified by its integration with algorithmic systems. Data alone does not exert control; it is the combination of data and algorithms that enables influence. Algorithms process data, identify patterns, and generate outputs that guide decisions. In this context, data serves as the input that fuels algorithmic processes, while algorithms act as the mechanisms that translate data into action. Together, they form a system capable of shaping behavior at scale.

This interplay between data and algorithms has significant implications for autonomy and agency. As systems become more adept at predicting and influencing behavior, the distinction between choice and suggestion becomes increasingly blurred. Individuals may perceive themselves as making independent decisions, while in reality, their options are being shaped by data-driven systems. This subtle form of influence is one of the defining features of the algorithmic age.

The concept of data as a currency of control also highlights the asymmetry that exists within digital systems. Not all entities have equal access to data or the ability to leverage it effectively. Large organizations with advanced analytical capabilities can extract significant value from data, while individuals often lack the tools to understand or utilize their own data. This imbalance creates a concentration of power, where those who control data hold a disproportionate influence over systems and outcomes.

In this context, data is not merely a technical resource—it is a strategic instrument. It underpins economic models, shapes technological systems, and influences social dynamics. Its value extends beyond its informational content to its capacity to enable control and coordination. As such, understanding the role of data is essential to understanding the broader structure of the algorithmic dictatorship.

This chapter explores the nature of data as a currency of control, examining how it is collected, processed, and utilized within modern systems. It seeks to uncover the mechanisms through which data exerts influence and to analyze the implications of its growing centrality. In doing so, it provides a foundation for understanding the power dynamics that define the digital age—where information is not just knowledge, but control.

The Data Extraction Economy

The data extraction economy represents a fundamental reconfiguration of how value is created, accumulated, and controlled in the digital age. Unlike traditional economic systems, which rely on the production and exchange of goods and services, the data extraction economy is built on the continuous harvesting of information. It transforms human activity into a resource, converting behavior, preferences, and interactions into data that can be analyzed, monetized, and leveraged for influence. In this system, individuals are not merely consumers or participants; they are sources of raw material.

At its core, the data extraction economy operates on a simple premise: every digital interaction has value. When individuals browse websites, engage with social media, make purchases, or even move through physical spaces with connected devices, they generate data. This data is not incidental—it is systematically captured, stored, and analyzed by platforms and organizations. Over time, these data points accumulate into detailed profiles that reveal patterns of behavior, interests, and tendencies. These profiles become the foundation for a wide range of economic activities, from targeted advertising to predictive analytics.

The extraction of data is often invisible to those who generate it. Unlike traditional forms of resource extraction, which involve physical processes such as mining or drilling, data extraction occurs through digital interfaces and automated systems. Users interact with platforms that appear to provide free services—social networking, search engines, navigation tools—but in reality, these services are part of a broader exchange. The cost is not monetary, but informational. Users provide data in return for access, often without fully understanding the extent of the exchange.

This asymmetry of awareness is a defining feature of the data extraction economy. Organizations that collect data possess sophisticated tools and expertise to analyze and utilize it, while individuals typically have limited visibility into how their data is used. This creates an imbalance of power, where the entities that control data can derive significant value from it, while those who generate it receive limited direct benefit. The result is a system in which value flows disproportionately toward those who have the capacity to collect and process data at scale.

The mechanisms of data extraction are diverse and continuously evolving. At a basic level, data is collected through user interactions—clicks, searches, and inputs. However, modern systems extend far beyond these explicit actions. Passive data collection captures information about browsing behavior, location, device usage, and even biometric signals. Cookies, tracking pixels, and embedded scripts monitor user activity across platforms, creating a comprehensive view of behavior over time. Mobile devices, equipped with sensors and connectivity, generate continuous streams of data about movement and environment. The proliferation of connected devices has expanded the scope of data extraction into the physical world, blurring the boundary between digital and real-life activity.

Once collected, data is aggregated and processed to extract meaningful insights. This process involves organizing data into structured formats, cleaning it to remove inconsistencies, and applying analytical models to identify patterns. Machine learning algorithms play a central role in this stage, enabling systems to detect correlations and make predictions based on historical data. These insights are then used to inform decisions, optimize processes, and create personalized experiences.

One of the most prominent applications of extracted data is targeted advertising. Advertising has long been a central component of economic systems, but the data extraction economy has transformed its nature. Instead of broadcasting messages to broad audiences, advertisers can now target specific individuals based on detailed profiles. Data allows for the segmentation of audiences into highly specific categories, enabling personalized messaging that is more likely to resonate. This precision increases the effectiveness of advertising, making it a highly profitable use of data.

However, the value of data extends beyond advertising. In many industries, data is used to optimize operations and drive innovation. In retail, data informs inventory management, pricing strategies, and customer engagement. In finance, it is used to assess risk, detect fraud, and guide investment decisions. In healthcare, data supports diagnosis, treatment planning, and research. In each case, the ability to extract and analyze data provides a competitive advantage, allowing organizations to operate more efficiently and effectively.

The data extraction economy also gives rise to new business models. Platforms that collect and analyze data become intermediaries, connecting users, advertisers, and service providers. These platforms operate as ecosystems, where interactions generate data that feeds back into the system. The more users a platform has, the more data it can collect, and the more valuable it becomes. This creates a network effect, where growth leads to increased value, which in turn attracts more users. Over time, this dynamic can lead to the concentration of power in a small number of dominant platforms.

This concentration raises important questions about competition and control. When a few entities control large volumes of data, they gain significant influence over markets and systems. They can shape user experiences, determine access to information, and set the terms of engagement for other participants. This influence extends beyond economic considerations, affecting social and political dynamics as well. The ability to control data becomes a form of power, one that is exercised through algorithms and platforms rather than traditional institutions.

The data extraction economy also has implications for privacy and autonomy. As data collection becomes more pervasive, individuals may have limited control over their personal information. Data is often collected without explicit consent or with consent that is not fully informed. Privacy policies and terms of service are frequently complex and difficult to understand, making it challenging for users to make informed decisions about data sharing. This lack of transparency undermines the notion of voluntary participation, raising ethical concerns about the legitimacy of data extraction practices.

Moreover, the continuous extraction of data can lead to a form of behavioral monitoring that affects how individuals act. When people are aware that their actions are being tracked, they may alter their behavior, consciously or unconsciously. This phenomenon, often referred to as the "observer effect," highlights the broader impact of data extraction on human experience. It is not only about what is collected, but how the act of collection itself influences behavior.

Another critical aspect of the data extraction economy is the commodification of human experience. Activities that were once private or ephemeral are now transformed into data points that can be analyzed and monetized. Social interactions, preferences, and even emotions become part of a dataset. This commodification raises questions about the boundaries between personal life and economic activity. When every action can be measured and valued, the distinction between living and producing becomes blurred.

The sustainability of the data extraction economy is also a subject of debate. While data provides significant value, its extraction and processing require substantial resources, including energy and infrastructure. Data centers, which store and process vast amounts of information, consume large amounts of electricity and contribute to environmental impact. As the volume of data continues to grow, these considerations become increasingly important.

In response to these challenges, there is a growing movement toward greater regulation and accountability. Governments and institutions are exploring ways to protect privacy, ensure transparency, and promote fair competition. Data protection laws, such as those that regulate how data is collected and used, aim to give individuals more control over their information. However, the global and rapidly evolving nature of the data extraction economy makes regulation complex and often fragmented.

In conclusion, the data extraction economy represents a shift in how value is generated and distributed. It transforms human activity into a resource, enabling new forms of economic activity and influence. While it offers significant benefits in terms of efficiency, personalization, and innovation, it also introduces challenges related to power, privacy, and ethics. Understanding this economy is essential for navigating the algorithmic age, as it underpins many of the systems that shape modern life.

Ultimately, the data extraction economy is not just about technology—it is about the redefinition of value itself. In a world where data is the primary resource, control over information becomes synonymous with control over systems, decisions, and outcomes.

Behavioural Data and Digital Footprints

In the architecture of the modern digital ecosystem, behavioral data has emerged as one of the most valuable and influential forms of information. Unlike traditional data, which often captures static attributes such as age, location, or income, behavioral data reflects actions—what people do, how they interact, and how they respond to stimuli. It is dynamic, continuously generated, and deeply revealing. When aggregated over time, it forms what is commonly referred to as a digital footprint: a detailed and evolving record of an individual's presence and activity across digital environments.

A digital footprint is not a single entity but a composite of multiple layers of data. It includes explicit data, such as information users knowingly provide—profiles, posts, messages—as well as implicit data, which is collected through observation of behavior. Every click, scroll, pause, search query, purchase, and interaction contributes to this footprint. Even seemingly insignificant actions, when combined and analyzed at scale, can reveal patterns that provide insight into preferences, habits, and tendencies. Over time, these patterns become increasingly precise, allowing systems to construct detailed behavioral profiles.

The distinction between explicit and implicit data is critical to understanding the nature of behavioral data. Explicit data is often shared voluntarily and with awareness. Users know they are providing information when they fill out a form or post content. Implicit data, however, is collected passively, often without direct awareness. For example, the amount of time a user spends viewing a particular piece of content, the speed at which they scroll, or the sequence of actions they take on a platform can all be tracked and analyzed. This passive collection enables systems to capture a more authentic representation of behavior, as it reflects actions rather than stated intentions.

The value of behavioral data lies in its predictive power. While demographic data can provide general insights, behavioral data offers a more granular and accurate understanding of individuals. It reveals not just who people are, but how they behave in different contexts. This allows systems to anticipate future actions with a high degree of accuracy. For instance, by analyzing past purchasing behavior, a system can predict what products a user is likely to buy. By examining engagement patterns, it can determine what type of content will capture attention. This predictive capability transforms behavioral data into a powerful tool for decision-making and influence.

Digital footprints are not confined to a single platform or environment. In many cases, they extend across multiple systems, creating a comprehensive view of an individual's activity. Cross-platform tracking technologies enable the aggregation of data from different sources, linking interactions across websites, applications, and devices. This integration allows for a more holistic understanding of behavior, as it captures the continuity of actions across contexts. A user's activity on a social media platform, for example, can be connected to their browsing behavior on other websites, creating a unified profile that reflects their interests and preferences.

The expansion of connected devices has further amplified the scope of digital footprints. Smartphones, wearable devices, smart home systems, and other Internet of Things (IoT) technologies generate continuous streams of data about physical activity, location, and environment. This extends the concept of the digital footprint beyond the virtual realm into the physical world. Movement patterns, daily routines, and even physiological signals can become part of a behavioral dataset. The boundary between online and offline behavior becomes increasingly blurred, as both are captured and integrated into a single data ecosystem.

One of the defining characteristics of digital footprints is their persistence. Unlike traditional interactions, which may leave no lasting record, digital actions are often stored indefinitely. Data can be archived, replicated, and analyzed long after the original interaction has occurred. This persistence allows for longitudinal analysis, where behavior is studied over extended periods. Patterns that may not be visible in short-term data become apparent when viewed over time. This temporal dimension enhances the predictive power of behavioral data, as it captures not just isolated actions, but trends and trajectories.

However, the persistence of digital footprints also raises significant concerns. Information that was generated in one context may be used in another, potentially leading to unintended consequences. Past behavior can influence future opportunities, as data-driven systems use historical information to make decisions. For example, a person's digital footprint may affect their eligibility for financial services, employment opportunities, or access to certain platforms. This introduces a form of continuity where past actions are perpetually relevant, reducing the possibility of anonymity or reinvention.

The aggregation of behavioral data into digital footprints enables a process known as profiling. Profiling involves analyzing data to categorize individuals based on their characteristics and behavior. These profiles are used to segment populations, identify target audiences, and tailor experiences. In commercial contexts, profiling allows for personalized recommendations and targeted advertising. In other domains, such as security or governance, it can be used to assess risk or monitor activity. While profiling can enhance efficiency and relevance, it also introduces the potential for bias and discrimination.

Behavioral data is inherently probabilistic. It does not provide certainty about individual actions, but rather estimates based on patterns and correlations. This means that digital footprints are not perfect representations of individuals, but approximations constructed from data. These approximations can be highly accurate, but they are not infallible. Errors, biases, and incomplete data can lead to incorrect conclusions. Despite this, decisions are often made based on these profiles, highlighting the importance of understanding their limitations.

The influence of behavioral data extends beyond prediction to shaping behavior itself. Systems that analyze digital footprints often use this information to guide user interactions. Recommendation algorithms, for example, suggest content based on past behavior, creating a feedback loop where users are exposed to information that aligns with their existing preferences. This can reinforce patterns, making behavior more predictable over time. In this way, behavioral data not only reflects actions but also influences them, creating a dynamic interplay between observation and intervention.

Privacy is a central concern in the context of behavioral data and digital footprints. The collection and analysis of detailed behavioral information can intrude into personal aspects of life, raising questions about consent and control. Individuals may not fully understand the extent of data collection or how their data is used. Even when consent is obtained, it is often through complex agreements that are difficult to interpret. This creates a gap between the formal acknowledgment of data collection and the practical understanding of its implications.

Another important aspect is the issue of data ownership. While individuals generate behavioral data through their actions, the data is typically collected and controlled by organizations. This creates a situation where the value derived from data is not necessarily shared with those who produce it. The question of who owns digital footprints—and who has the right to use them—remains a topic of ongoing debate. Some advocate for greater user control and data portability, while others emphasize the role of organizations in managing and securing data.

The ethical implications of behavioral data are complex and multifaceted. On one hand, the use of data can enhance user experiences, improve services, and drive innovation. On the other hand, it can lead to manipulation, surveillance, and loss of autonomy. The ability to predict and influence behavior raises questions about the balance between personalization and control. When systems know what users are likely to do, they can guide them toward specific actions, potentially limiting the range of choices.

In conclusion, behavioral data and digital footprints are central to the functioning of modern digital systems. They provide the raw material for analysis, prediction, and influence, enabling systems to operate with a high degree of precision. At the same time, they introduce challenges related to privacy, ownership, and ethics. As digital footprints become more comprehensive and persistent, their impact on individuals and society will continue to grow.

Understanding behavioral data is essential for navigating the algorithmic age. It reveals how actions are transformed into information, how information is used to shape systems, and how those systems, in turn, influence behavior. In this interconnected cycle, digital footprints are not just records of the past—they are instruments of the future.

Surveillance Capitalism Explained

Surveillance capitalism is a term used to describe a new economic system in which personal data is collected, analyzed, and monetized at an unprecedented scale. It represents a shift from traditional market dynamics toward a model where human experience itself becomes a source of raw material. In this system, everyday activities—communication, browsing, movement, and interaction—are continuously monitored and transformed into data. This data is then used to predict, influence, and ultimately shape behavior for economic gain. Unlike earlier forms of capitalism that relied on the production of goods or services, surveillance capitalism is centered on the extraction and utilization of behavioral data.

At the core of surveillance capitalism is the concept of data as a commodity. However, unlike physical commodities, data is not inherently scarce. It is generated continuously and can be replicated without loss. Its value lies not in its existence, but in its potential to reveal patterns and enable predictions. Companies operating within this framework collect vast amounts of data from users, often through digital platforms that provide services such as search, social networking, or e-commerce. These services are typically offered at little or no direct cost, creating the perception of free access. In reality, users are paying with their data, which becomes the foundation for the platform's revenue model.

The process begins with data collection. Every interaction within a digital environment generates data points. These include explicit actions, such as clicks and searches, as well as implicit signals, such as time spent on content, scrolling behavior, and even cursor movements. Advanced tracking technologies extend this collection beyond individual platforms, enabling the aggregation of data across multiple websites and applications. This creates a comprehensive profile of user behavior, capturing not only what individuals do, but how and when they do it.

Once collected, this data undergoes processing and analysis. Machine learning algorithms are applied to identify patterns, correlations, and trends within the data. These patterns are used to construct predictive models that estimate future behavior. For example, a system may predict which products a user is likely to purchase, what content they will engage with, or how they might respond to a particular message. These predictions are not deterministic; they are probabilistic, based on statistical relationships within the data. However, when applied at scale, they can achieve a high degree of accuracy.

The monetization of these predictions is a defining feature of surveillance capitalism. One of the primary mechanisms for this is targeted advertising. Advertisers seek to reach specific audiences with messages that are likely to influence behavior. Data-driven platforms enable this by providing detailed audience segmentation and precise targeting capabilities. Advertisements can be tailored to individual users based on their profiles, increasing the likelihood of engagement and conversion. In this way, data is transformed into a revenue-generating asset.

However, the influence of surveillance capitalism extends beyond advertising. Predictive models are used in a wide range of applications, from recommendation systems to dynamic pricing strategies. In e-commerce, for example, platforms may adjust prices based on perceived willingness to pay, inferred from user behavior. In content platforms, algorithms prioritize certain types of information to maximize engagement. These practices demonstrate how data-driven insights are used not only to predict behavior but to shape it.

A key characteristic of surveillance capitalism is its asymmetry. The entities that collect and analyze data possess extensive knowledge about users, while users have limited visibility into how their data is used. This imbalance creates a concentration of power, where a small number of organizations control vast amounts of information. These organizations have the capability to influence markets, shape public discourse, and guide individual behavior. The lack of transparency in these processes makes it difficult for users to understand or challenge the systems that affect them.

The concept of surveillance in this context does not necessarily imply intentional monitoring by a human observer. Instead, it refers to the continuous and automated collection of data through technological systems. This form of surveillance is embedded in the infrastructure of digital platforms, operating as a default feature rather than an explicit action. Users may not perceive themselves as being surveilled, as the process is integrated into the functionality of the services they use. This normalization of data collection is a defining aspect of surveillance capitalism.

Another important dimension is the transformation of human behavior into a resource. In traditional economic systems, resources are typically external to individuals—natural materials, labor, or capital. In surveillance capitalism, the resource is internal: it is the behavior of individuals themselves. This behavior is extracted, analyzed, and converted into value. The more data a system can collect, the more accurate its predictions become, and the more valuable it is. This creates an incentive to maximize data collection, often extending beyond what is necessary for the provision of services.

The feedback loop created by surveillance capitalism further amplifies its influence. Predictions generated by data analysis are used to shape user experiences, which in turn influence behavior. This behavior generates new data, which is fed back into the system to refine future predictions. Over time, this cycle can lead to increasingly precise models of behavior. It also means that systems are not merely observing behavior but actively participating in its formation.

The ethical implications of surveillance capitalism are significant. Privacy is one of the primary concerns. The extensive collection of personal data raises questions about consent and control. Users may not fully understand what data is being collected or how it is used. Even when consent is obtained, it is often through complex agreements that are difficult to interpret. This creates a situation where individuals have limited agency over their own information.

Bias and fairness are also critical issues. Predictive models are trained on historical data, which may reflect existing inequalities or biases. If these biases are not addressed, they can be perpetuated or amplified by the system. This can lead to discriminatory outcomes in areas such as employment, lending, or law enforcement. Ensuring fairness in data-driven systems requires careful consideration of data quality, model design, and evaluation processes.

The impact of surveillance capitalism on autonomy is another area of concern. As systems become more capable of predicting and influencing behavior, the line between choice and manipulation becomes less clear. Users may be guided toward certain actions through personalized recommendations or targeted messaging. While these interventions are often subtle, they can shape decision-making in significant ways. This raises questions about the extent to which individuals retain control over their own choices.

Regulation and governance are ongoing challenges in addressing the implications of surveillance capitalism. Governments and institutions are exploring ways to protect privacy, ensure transparency, and promote accountability. Data protection laws aim to give individuals more control over their information, while regulatory frameworks seek to address issues such as market dominance and unfair practices. However, the global nature of digital platforms and the rapid pace of technological change make regulation complex and often fragmented.

Despite these challenges, surveillance capitalism continues to expand. Advances in technology, including artificial intelligence and the Internet of Things, are increasing the scope and depth of data collection. New forms of data, such as biometric and environmental information, are being integrated into existing systems. This expansion further embeds surveillance capitalism into the infrastructure of modern life, making it a central feature of the digital economy.

In conclusion, surveillance capitalism represents a new phase in the evolution of economic systems. It is characterized by the extraction of behavioral data, the use of predictive models, and the monetization of insights derived from that data. While it offers significant benefits in terms of efficiency, personalization, and innovation, it also introduces challenges related to privacy, power, and ethics. Understanding this system is essential for navigating the complexities of the algorithmic age.

Ultimately, surveillance capitalism is not just about technology or economics—it is about the relationship between individuals and systems. It raises fundamental questions about how data is used, who controls it, and what it means for autonomy and freedom in a world where behavior itself has become a commodity.

Ownership, Consent, and Exploitation

In the data-driven architecture of the modern digital economy, the concepts of ownership, consent, and exploitation form a critical triad that defines the relationship between individuals and the systems they engage with. As data becomes the primary currency of value, questions surrounding who owns that data, how consent is obtained, and whether the extraction of data constitutes exploitation have moved from the margins of technical discourse to the center of ethical, legal, and societal debate. These questions are not merely theoretical—they shape the dynamics of power, control, and agency in the algorithmic age.

Ownership, in its traditional sense, implies control, authority, and the right to benefit from a resource. In physical economies, ownership is relatively straightforward. Assets such as land, goods, or intellectual property can be clearly defined, transferred, and protected through established legal frameworks. However, in the realm of data, ownership becomes far more complex. Data is not a static object; it is generated through interactions, often involving multiple parties and systems. For example, when a user interacts with a digital platform, the resulting data is a product of both the user's actions and the platform's infrastructure. This shared origin complicates the notion of ownership.

In many cases, individuals generate data through their behavior, yet they do not retain control over it. Instead, the platforms that collect and store the data assert ownership or, at the very least, control over its use. This control is often established through terms of service agreements, which grant platforms broad rights to collect, analyze, and monetize user data. These agreements are typically presented as a condition of access, leaving users with limited options: accept the terms or forgo the service. As a result, ownership in the digital context is often less about who creates the data and more about who has the capacity to control and utilize it.

This asymmetry in ownership is closely tied to the concept of consent. In principle, consent is intended to provide individuals with the ability to make informed decisions about how their data is used. It is a mechanism designed to ensure that data collection and processing occur with the user's knowledge and agreement. In practice, however, consent in the digital environment is frequently ambiguous and constrained. Users are often presented with lengthy and complex privacy policies that are difficult to understand. The act of consenting becomes a procedural formality rather than a meaningful choice.

Moreover, consent is often bundled with access. Digital platforms typically operate on a model where services are contingent upon agreement to data collection practices. This creates a situation where consent is not entirely voluntary, as declining to consent may result in exclusion from essential services. In such cases, the notion of informed consent is undermined, as users may feel compelled to agree without fully understanding or accepting the implications. The imbalance of power between users and platforms further complicates this dynamic, as users have limited ability to negotiate terms or influence how their data is handled.

The issue of exploitation arises when the extraction and use of data generate value that is not equitably shared with those who produce it. In the data extraction economy, individuals contribute data through their interactions, yet the economic benefits derived from that data are largely captured by organizations. This creates a form of value transfer, where the output of individual behavior is converted into profit without direct compensation. While users receive services in exchange, the value of these services may not correspond to the value generated by their data.

Exploitation in this context is not always overt or intentional. It often emerges from systemic dynamics rather than explicit actions. The design of digital platforms encourages engagement, which in turn generates data. This engagement is facilitated through features that are optimized to capture attention and prolong interaction. As users spend more time on platforms, they produce more data, increasing the value that can be extracted. This cycle creates an incentive for platforms to maximize data collection, sometimes at the expense of user autonomy or well-being.

The concept of exploitation also extends to the use of data for behavioral influence. When data is used to predict and shape behavior, it introduces a layer of control that may not be fully transparent to users. For example, targeted advertising and personalized content are designed to influence decisions and preferences. While these practices can enhance user experience, they also raise questions about manipulation and autonomy. If users are guided toward certain actions based on data-driven insights, the extent to which those actions are truly independent becomes uncertain.

Another dimension of exploitation is the unequal distribution of risks and benefits. While organizations benefit from the use of data, individuals may bear the risks associated with data breaches, misuse, or unintended consequences. Personal data, once collected, can be vulnerable to unauthorized access or exploitation. The impact of such events can be significant, affecting privacy, security, and reputation. Yet, the responsibility for managing these risks is often not proportionally shared between users and organizations.

The interplay between ownership, consent, and exploitation is further complicated by the global nature of digital systems. Data flows across borders, subject to different legal frameworks and regulatory standards. This creates challenges in establishing consistent rules for data governance. Some jurisdictions have introduced regulations aimed at enhancing user rights, such as the ability to access, correct, or delete personal data. These measures represent attempts to rebalance the relationship between users and platforms, but their effectiveness varies depending on implementation and enforcement.

Technological developments also influence this dynamic. Advances in artificial intelligence and data analytics increase the capacity to extract value from data, intensifying the incentives for data collection. At the same time, new technologies such as decentralized systems and privacy-enhancing tools offer potential avenues for greater user control. These innovations suggest that the current model of data ownership and consent is not fixed, but subject to evolution.

The ethical considerations surrounding ownership, consent, and exploitation are central to the broader discourse on the algorithmic age. They raise fundamental questions about fairness, autonomy, and the distribution of power. Should individuals have greater control over their data? How can consent be made more meaningful and informed? What mechanisms can ensure that the benefits of data-driven systems are more equitably distributed? These questions do not have simple answers, but they are essential for shaping the future of digital systems.

From a societal perspective, the implications are profound. The way data is governed affects not only individual experiences but also collective outcomes. Data-driven systems influence economic opportunities, access to information, and social dynamics. If ownership and control remain concentrated, the resulting power imbalance may have far-reaching consequences. Conversely, more equitable models of data governance could enable broader participation and benefit.

In conclusion, the issues of ownership, consent, and exploitation are deeply intertwined within the data-driven economy. They define the terms under which individuals interact with digital systems and determine how value is created and distributed. As data continues to play a central role in shaping modern society, addressing these issues becomes increasingly important. It requires a combination of technological innovation, regulatory frameworks, and ethical consideration.

Ultimately, the challenge is to create a system where data serves not only as a source of value but also as a foundation for trust and fairness. This involves rethinking how ownership is defined, how consent is obtained, and how the benefits of data are shared. In doing so, it is possible to move toward a more balanced and transparent digital ecosystem—one where the currency of control is aligned with the principles of equity and accountability.

Chapter 3

The Architecture of Algorithms

In the modern digital landscape, algorithms are often described in functional terms—as tools that sort, rank, recommend, or predict. Yet beneath these surface-level functions lies a deeper reality: algorithms are not just operational mechanisms; they are structured systems of logic that shape how decisions are made, how information flows, and how outcomes are determined. To understand their influence, it is necessary to move beyond what algorithms do and examine how they are built. This underlying structure—the architecture of algorithms—defines their capabilities, limitations, and impact.

At its core, an algorithm is a set of instructions designed to process inputs and produce outputs. However, in contemporary systems, this definition is only the starting point. Modern algorithms are rarely simple or linear. They are composed of multiple layers, interconnected components, and dynamic processes that operate simultaneously. These systems are designed not only to execute tasks but to adapt, optimize, and evolve over time. Their architecture reflects a shift from static rule-based logic to complex, data-driven frameworks.

The architecture of an algorithm determines how it interprets data, how it prioritizes variables, and how it generates results. This structure is not neutral. Every design choice—what data is included, how it is weighted, what objectives are optimized—introduces a set of assumptions and values into the system. These choices influence the behavior of the algorithm and, by extension, the outcomes it produces. In this sense, algorithms embed human decisions within technical systems, translating abstract goals into operational rules.

One of the defining features of modern algorithmic architecture is its reliance on data as a foundational element. Unlike traditional systems, where logic is explicitly defined by programmers, many contemporary algorithms derive their behavior from data. Machine learning models, for example, are trained on datasets that shape how they interpret new inputs. The architecture of these systems includes not only the computational model but also the data pipeline—how data is collected, processed, and integrated. The quality, diversity, and structure of this data have a direct impact on the performance and fairness of the algorithm.

Another critical aspect of algorithmic architecture is its modularity. Complex systems are often composed of multiple modules, each responsible for a specific function. These modules interact with one another, passing information and influencing outcomes. For example, a recommendation system may include components for data collection, feature extraction, model training, and output generation. Each component operates within its own framework, yet contributes to the overall behavior of the system. This modular design allows for scalability and flexibility, but it also introduces complexity, making it more difficult to understand how the system functions as a whole.

The increasing use of machine learning has further transformed algorithmic architecture. In traditional programming, the logic of an algorithm is explicitly defined and transparent. In contrast, machine learning models often operate as adaptive systems, where the internal logic is derived from patterns in data. This results in architectures that are less interpretable, sometimes referred to as "black boxes." While these systems can achieve high levels of accuracy, their lack of transparency raises important questions about accountability and trust. Understanding how decisions are made becomes more challenging when the underlying processes are not easily observable.

Optimization is another central principle in algorithmic architecture. Algorithms are typically designed to achieve specific objectives, such as maximizing engagement, minimizing error, or improving efficiency. These objectives are encoded into the system as optimization functions, which guide how the algorithm processes data and selects outcomes. The choice of objective has significant implications. For instance, an algorithm optimized for engagement may prioritize content that captures attention, regardless of its accuracy or quality. This highlights the importance of aligning algorithmic objectives with broader societal values.

The architecture of algorithms also reflects the environments in which they operate. Systems designed for large-scale platforms must handle vast amounts of data and serve millions of users simultaneously. This requires distributed architectures, where processing is spread across multiple systems and locations. Such architectures enable scalability and resilience, but they also add layers of complexity. The interactions between different components can produce emergent behaviors that are not easily predicted or controlled.

Security and robustness are additional considerations in algorithmic design. As algorithms become integral to critical systems, ensuring their reliability and resistance to manipulation becomes essential. Adversarial inputs, data corruption, and system failures can all affect the performance of an algorithm. Designing architectures that can withstand these challenges requires careful planning and continuous monitoring. This adds another dimension to the architecture, where resilience is as important as functionality.

The significance of algorithmic architecture extends beyond technical considerations. It shapes how information is presented, how decisions are made, and how individuals interact with systems. In many cases, users are unaware of the underlying architecture, yet it influences their experiences and choices. The ranking of search results, the content displayed in feeds, and the recommendations provided by platforms are all outcomes of algorithmic structures. These structures act as intermediaries between users and information, filtering and prioritizing what is seen and what is not.

As algorithms become more pervasive, their architecture becomes a critical factor in understanding their role in society. It is not enough to evaluate algorithms based on their outputs; it is necessary to examine how those outputs are generated. This involves analyzing the design principles, data dependencies, and optimization strategies that define the system. By doing so, it becomes possible to identify potential biases, limitations, and areas for improvement.

This chapter explores the architecture of algorithms, focusing on how they are designed, how they operate, and how they influence outcomes. It examines the components and principles that underpin algorithmic systems, providing a framework for understanding their complexity. By unpacking the structure of algorithms, we can gain insight into the mechanisms that drive the algorithmic age—and the ways in which these systems shape the world around us.

How Algorithms Are Designed

The design of algorithms is a structured and deliberate process that transforms abstract objectives into operational systems capable of processing data and producing outcomes. While algorithms are often perceived as neutral tools, their design reflects a series of choices, assumptions, and priorities that shape how they function. Understanding how algorithms are designed requires examining the stages through which they are conceptualized, developed, tested, and deployed. Each stage contributes to the behavior of the system and determines how it interacts with data, users, and environments.

The design process begins with problem definition. Before an algorithm can be created, the problem it is intended to solve must be clearly articulated. This involves identifying the objectives, constraints, and desired outcomes. For example, an algorithm designed to recommend content must define what constitutes a "good" recommendation. Is it based on user engagement, relevance, diversity, or accuracy? These criteria are not inherently technical; they are conceptual decisions that guide the design process. The way a problem is framed influences every subsequent step, determining what data is used, how it is processed, and what outcomes are prioritized.

Once the problem is defined, the next step is data selection and preparation. Data serves as the foundation upon which algorithms operate. Designers must determine what data is relevant, how it will be collected, and how it will be structured. This stage involves sourcing data from various channels, cleaning it to remove errors or inconsistencies, and transforming it into a format suitable for analysis. The quality and representativeness of the data are critical, as they directly affect the performance and fairness of the algorithm. If the data is incomplete or biased, the algorithm may produce skewed results, reinforcing existing patterns rather than providing objective insights.

Feature engineering is another essential component of algorithm design. Features are the variables or attributes that the algorithm uses to make decisions. In many cases, raw data must be transformed into meaningful features that capture relevant aspects of the problem. For instance, in a recommendation system, features might include user preferences, interaction history, and contextual information such as time or location. The selection and construction of features require both technical expertise and domain knowledge, as they determine how the algorithm interprets the data.

With the data prepared and features defined, the design process moves to model selection. This involves choosing the type of algorithmic model that will be used to solve the problem. There are various classes of algorithms, each suited to different types of tasks. Rule-based algorithms follow explicit instructions and are often used in deterministic environments. Statistical models rely on mathematical relationships within data to make predictions. Machine learning models, particularly those based on neural networks, can learn complex patterns from data and adapt over time. The choice of model depends on factors such as the complexity of the problem, the nature of the data, and the desired level of accuracy.

Model training is a critical phase in the design of data-driven algorithms. During this stage, the algorithm is exposed to a dataset and learns to identify patterns and relationships. In supervised learning, the model is trained on labeled data, where the correct outcomes are known. The algorithm adjusts its internal parameters to minimize the difference between its predictions and the actual outcomes. In unsupervised learning, the model identifies patterns without predefined labels, discovering structures within the data. The training process often involves iterative optimization, where the model is repeatedly refined to improve performance.

Evaluation and validation are essential to ensure that the algorithm performs as intended. Designers use various metrics to assess the accuracy, efficiency, and robustness of the model. These metrics may include measures such as precision, recall, and error rates. Validation involves testing the model on data that was not used during training, providing an indication of how it will perform in real-world scenarios. This step is crucial for identifying issues such as overfitting, where the model performs well on training data but fails to generalize to new data.

Optimization is an ongoing aspect of algorithm design. Once a model is developed, designers may refine it to improve performance. This can involve adjusting parameters, selecting different features, or experimenting with alternative models. Optimization is guided by the objectives defined at the outset, such as maximizing accuracy or minimizing computational cost. However, optimizing for one objective may impact others. For example, increasing accuracy may require more complex models, which can reduce interpretability or increase processing time. Designers must balance these trade-offs to achieve the desired outcomes.

Another important consideration in algorithm design is interpretability. In some applications, it is essential to understand how the algorithm arrives at its decisions. This is particularly important in high-stakes domains such as healthcare, finance, and law. Interpretable models provide insights into the factors that influence outcomes, enabling users to trust and verify the system. However, there is often a trade-off between interpretability and complexity. More sophisticated models may achieve higher accuracy but operate as "black boxes," making their internal logic difficult to explain.

Deployment is the stage where the algorithm is integrated into a real-world system. This involves embedding the model within an application or platform, where it can process live data and generate outputs. Deployment requires consideration of factors such as scalability, latency, and reliability. The algorithm must be capable of handling large volumes of data and delivering results within acceptable timeframes. It must also be robust to variations in input and resilient to potential failures.

Monitoring and maintenance are ongoing aspects of algorithm design. Once deployed, algorithms operate in dynamic environments where conditions can change over time. Data distributions may shift, user behavior may evolve, and new patterns may emerge. These changes can affect the performance of the algorithm, necessitating continuous monitoring and updates. Designers may retrain models with new data, adjust parameters, or modify features to maintain accuracy and relevance.

Ethical considerations are increasingly integral to the design of algorithms. Designers must consider the potential impact of their systems on individuals and society. This includes addressing issues such as bias, fairness, and privacy. Bias can arise from data, model design, or feature selection, leading to unequal outcomes for different groups. Ensuring fairness requires careful analysis and, in some cases, the implementation of corrective measures. Privacy considerations involve determining how data is collected, stored, and used, ensuring that individuals' rights are respected.

Security is another critical aspect of algorithm design. Algorithms must be protected against malicious attacks, such as adversarial inputs designed to manipulate outputs. Ensuring security involves implementing safeguards, testing for vulnerabilities, and continuously updating systems to address emerging threats. As algorithms become more central to critical systems, their security becomes a matter of significant importance.

The design of algorithms is not a one-time process but a continuous cycle of development, evaluation, and refinement. It involves collaboration between technical experts, domain specialists, and stakeholders. Each decision made during the design process contributes to the behavior of the algorithm and its impact on users and systems. Understanding this process reveals that algorithms are not neutral entities; they are constructed systems shaped by human choices and values.

In conclusion, the design of algorithms is a complex and multifaceted process that extends beyond technical implementation. It involves defining problems, selecting and preparing data, choosing models, training and evaluating systems, and considering ethical and practical implications. Each stage plays a critical role in determining how the algorithm functions and what outcomes it produces. As algorithms become increasingly integrated into everyday life, understanding how they are designed becomes essential for assessing their influence and ensuring that they serve broader societal goals.

Machine Learning and Neural Networks

Machine learning and neural networks represent a pivotal transformation in the evolution of algorithms—from systems that follow explicitly defined instructions to systems that learn from data. This shift has redefined how problems are approached, how decisions are made, and how intelligence is operationalized within machines. Unlike traditional algorithms, which rely on predefined logic crafted by human programmers, machine learning systems derive their behavior from patterns in data. Neural networks, as a specialized class of machine learning models, extend this capability by enabling the analysis of complex, high-dimensional information through layered computational structures.

At its core, machine learning is a methodological framework that allows systems to improve their performance on a task through experience. This experience is encoded in data. Instead of being told exactly how to perform a task, a machine learning model is exposed to examples and learns to identify relationships between inputs and outputs. The goal is to generalize from this experience, enabling the system to make accurate predictions or decisions when presented with new, unseen data.

Machine learning can be broadly categorized into several paradigms, each defined by the nature of the data and the learning process. In supervised learning, the model is trained on labeled data, where each input is paired with a known output. The system learns by minimizing the difference between its predictions and the actual outcomes. This approach is commonly used in tasks such as classification and regression. In unsupervised learning, the model is given unlabeled data and tasked with identifying patterns or structures within it. Clustering and dimensionality reduction are typical applications of this paradigm. Reinforcement learning, another important category, involves learning through interaction with an environment, where the model receives feedback in the form of rewards or penalties based on its actions.

The effectiveness of machine learning depends heavily on data. The quantity, quality, and diversity of data directly influence the model's ability to learn and generalize. Large datasets provide more information for the model to identify patterns, while high-quality data ensures that these patterns are meaningful and representative. However, data is not inherently neutral. It reflects the conditions under which it was generated, including any biases or limitations present in the environment. As a result, machine learning models can inherit and amplify these biases, making data selection and preprocessing critical components of the learning process.

Neural networks represent one of the most advanced and widely used forms of machine learning. Inspired by the structure of the human brain, neural networks consist of interconnected layers of nodes, often referred to as neurons. Each neuron receives inputs, processes them through a mathematical function, and passes the result to the next layer. This layered architecture allows neural networks to model complex, non-linear relationships within data.

A typical neural network is composed of three main types of layers: input, hidden, and output. The input layer receives raw data, which is then transformed as it passes through one or more hidden layers. Each hidden layer extracts increasingly abstract features from the data. For example, in image recognition, early layers might detect simple patterns such as edges or colors, while deeper layers identify more complex structures such as shapes or objects. The output layer produces the final result, such as a classification or prediction.

The learning process in neural networks involves adjusting the weights associated with each connection between neurons. These weights determine the strength of the influence that one neuron has on another. During training, the network processes input data and generates predictions. The difference between the predicted and actual outcomes is measured using a loss function. The network then updates its weights to minimize this loss, typically through an optimization technique known as gradient descent. This iterative process continues until the model achieves an acceptable level of performance.

One of the defining features of neural networks is their ability to perform feature learning. In traditional machine learning approaches, features must often be manually engineered based on domain knowledge. Neural networks, however, can automatically learn relevant features from raw data. This capability makes them particularly effective in domains where the underlying structure of the data is complex or not well understood, such as natural language processing, image recognition, and speech analysis.

The rise of deep learning—a subset of machine learning that involves neural networks with many layers—has significantly expanded the capabilities of these systems. Deep neural networks can process vast amounts of data and model highly intricate relationships. This has led to breakthroughs in areas such as computer vision, where systems can recognize objects and faces with high accuracy, and natural language processing, where models can understand and generate human language.

Despite their power, neural networks are not without limitations. One of the primary challenges is their lack of interpretability. Unlike simpler models, where the relationship between inputs and outputs can be easily understood, neural networks often operate as "black boxes." The internal processes that lead to a particular decision are not always transparent, making it difficult to explain or justify outcomes. This lack of transparency can be problematic in applications where accountability and trust are essential.

Another challenge is the requirement for large amounts of data and computational resources. Training deep neural networks can be computationally intensive, requiring specialized hardware and significant energy consumption. This can limit accessibility and raise concerns about the environmental impact of large-scale machine learning systems. Additionally, models trained on large datasets may struggle to adapt to new or changing conditions, particularly if the data distribution shifts over time.

Bias and fairness are also critical considerations in machine learning and neural networks. Since these models learn from data, any biases present in the data can be reflected in the model's outputs. This can lead to unequal or discriminatory outcomes, particularly in sensitive applications such as hiring, lending, or law enforcement. Addressing these issues requires careful attention to data selection, model design, and evaluation processes, as well as ongoing monitoring and adjustment.

The integration of machine learning and neural networks into real-world systems has far-reaching implications. These technologies are increasingly used to automate decision-making processes, optimize operations, and enhance user experiences. In many cases, they operate behind the scenes, influencing outcomes without direct human intervention. This raises important questions about control, accountability, and the role of human oversight in algorithmic systems.

Furthermore, the adaptability of machine learning systems introduces a dynamic element to algorithmic behavior. Unlike static algorithms, which produce consistent outputs for given inputs, machine learning models can evolve over time as they are exposed to new data. This adaptability can improve performance but also introduces uncertainty, as the behavior of the system may change in ways that are not fully predictable.

In conclusion, machine learning and neural networks represent a fundamental shift in how algorithms are designed and implemented. They enable systems to learn from data, adapt to new information, and perform complex tasks that were previously beyond the reach of traditional programming. At the same time, they introduce challenges related to interpretability, bias, and resource requirements. Understanding these technologies is essential for navigating the algorithmic age, as they form the backbone of many systems that shape modern life.

Ultimately, machine learning and neural networks are not just technical tools, they are systems of transformation. They redefine the relationship between data and decision-making, enabling a level of automation and insight that continues to expand. As these systems become more pervasive, their influence will extend further into the structures that govern society, making it increasingly important to understand how they work and how they are applied.

Bias, Training Data, and Systemic Errors

In the architecture of modern algorithmic systems, bias is not an anomaly—it is an inherent risk embedded within the data, design, and deployment of these systems. While algorithms are often perceived as objective and impartial, their outputs are deeply influenced by the data they are trained on and the assumptions encoded within their structure. Bias, when unaddressed, can lead to systemic errors—patterns of inaccuracy or unfairness that are not isolated incidents but recurring outcomes across populations and contexts. Understanding how bias emerges, how training data shapes behavior, and how systemic errors propagate is essential to evaluating the reliability and fairness of algorithmic systems.

Bias in algorithms originates primarily from training data. Machine learning models learn by identifying patterns in data, and these patterns reflect the conditions under which the data was generated. If the data contains imbalances, omissions, or distortions, the model will internalize these characteristics. For example, if a dataset disproportionately represents certain groups or behaviors, the model may perform well for those groups while underperforming for others. This is not a flaw in the algorithm's logic but a consequence of the data it has been exposed to. The model does not distinguish between patterns that are representative and those that are biased; it treats all patterns as valid signals.

The process of data collection plays a critical role in shaping bias. Data is often collected from specific sources, environments, or populations, which may not be representative of broader contexts. For instance, data collected from a particular geographic region or demographic group may not generalize to others. Additionally, historical data may reflect existing social, economic, or institutional biases. When such data is used to train models, these biases can be perpetuated and even amplified. The algorithm, in effect, learns from the past and projects those patterns into the future.

Sampling bias is one of the most common forms of bias in training data. It occurs when certain groups or outcomes are overrepresented or underrepresented in the dataset. This imbalance can lead to skewed predictions, as the model has more information about some cases than others. Another form is measurement bias, which arises when the data used to represent a concept is inaccurate or incomplete. For example, using proxy variables that do not fully capture the intended attribute can introduce distortions. Labeling bias, where the labels assigned to data are subjective or inconsistent, can further compound these issues.

Beyond data, bias can also be introduced through the design of the algorithm itself. Designers make decisions about which features to include, how to weight them, and what objectives to optimize. These choices reflect implicit assumptions about what is important or relevant. For example, an algorithm optimized for efficiency may prioritize speed over fairness, leading to outcomes that disadvantage certain groups. Similarly, the selection of features may inadvertently encode sensitive attributes, such as race or gender, even if these attributes are not explicitly included. This occurs because other variables may correlate with these attributes, allowing the model to infer them indirectly.

Systemic errors emerge when bias is not only present but consistently affects outcomes across multiple instances. These errors are not random; they follow patterns that reflect the underlying biases in the system. For example, if an algorithm consistently underestimates the creditworthiness of a particular group, this constitutes a systemic error. Such errors can have significant consequences, affecting access to resources, opportunities, and services. Because they are embedded in the system, they can persist over time, reinforcing existing disparities.

One of the challenges in addressing bias and systemic errors is their subtlety. Unlike explicit discrimination, which can be directly observed and challenged, algorithmic bias often operates indirectly. It may not be immediately apparent that an outcome is biased, particularly when it is presented as the result of a neutral, data-driven process. This opacity makes it difficult to identify and correct biases, as the underlying mechanisms are not always transparent.

The feedback loop inherent in many algorithmic systems can exacerbate bias and systemic errors. When an algorithm's outputs influence future data, the system can reinforce its own patterns. For example, if a recommendation system consistently promotes certain types of content, users are more likely to engage with that content, generating data that supports the algorithm's initial assumptions. Over time, this can lead to a narrowing of diversity and the amplification of specific patterns. In such cases, bias is not only maintained but strengthened through repeated cycles.

Another important aspect is the distinction between individual and group fairness. An algorithm may perform accurately on average but still produce unequal outcomes for different groups. This raises questions about how fairness should be defined and measured. Should fairness be based on equal accuracy across groups, equal outcomes, or equal opportunities? These are not purely technical questions; they involve ethical considerations that must be addressed in the design and evaluation of algorithms.

Mitigating bias and systemic errors requires a multifaceted approach. One strategy is to improve the quality and diversity of training data. This involves ensuring that datasets are representative of the populations they are intended to serve and that they capture a wide range of scenarios. Data augmentation techniques can be used to address imbalances, while careful curation can help reduce the influence of biased or irrelevant data. However, improving data alone is not sufficient, as bias can also arise from other aspects of the system.

Algorithmic techniques can be employed to detect and mitigate bias. These include methods for fairness-aware learning, which incorporate fairness constraints into the training process. For example, models can be designed to minimize disparities in outcomes across groups or to ensure that predictions are not influenced by sensitive attributes. Post-processing techniques can adjust outputs to correct for bias, while pre-processing methods can modify data before training to reduce imbalances. Each of these approaches has its own advantages and limitations, and their effectiveness depends on the specific context.

Transparency and interpretability are also crucial in addressing bias and systemic errors. By making the decision-making process of algorithms more understandable, it becomes easier to identify potential sources of bias and evaluate their impact. Explainable AI techniques aim to provide insights into how models arrive at their decisions, highlighting the factors that influence outcomes. While achieving full transparency in complex models is challenging, even partial insights can be valuable for accountability and trust.

Human oversight remains an essential component of bias mitigation. Algorithms should not be viewed as autonomous systems operating in isolation, but as tools that require monitoring and intervention. Regular audits, testing, and evaluation can help identify issues and ensure that systems perform as intended. Involving diverse perspectives in the design and evaluation process can also help uncover biases that may not be apparent to a homogeneous group of designers.

Regulatory frameworks and ethical guidelines play a role in shaping how bias is addressed. Policies that require transparency, accountability, and fairness can create incentives for organizations to prioritize these considerations. Standards for data governance, model evaluation, and reporting can help establish best practices and ensure consistency. However, regulation must be adaptable, as the rapid pace of technological change can outstrip static rules.

Despite these efforts, eliminating bias entirely may not be possible. Bias is often a reflection of broader societal conditions, and algorithms operate within these contexts. The goal, therefore, is not to achieve perfect neutrality, but to minimize harm and ensure that systems are as fair and equitable as possible. This requires ongoing vigilance, as new data, environments, and applications can introduce new forms of bias.

In conclusion, bias, training data, and systemic errors are deeply interconnected elements of algorithmic systems. Training data shapes the patterns that models learn, bias influences how these patterns are interpreted, and systemic errors reflect the cumulative impact of these factors. Addressing these challenges requires a comprehensive approach that combines technical, ethical, and organizational strategies. As algorithms continue to play a central role in decision-making, understanding and mitigating bias becomes essential for ensuring that these systems serve the broader interests of society.

Ultimately, the presence of bias in algorithms is not just a technical issue, it reflects how systems are designed and the values they embody. Recognizing this connection is the first step toward creating systems that are not only effective but also just.

Black Boxes and Lack of Transparency

As algorithmic systems grow more sophisticated, a defining challenge has emerged at the intersection of technology, governance, and trust: the problem of the "black box." In this context, a black box refers to a system whose internal workings are not easily observable or understandable, even when its inputs and outputs are visible. Modern machine learning models—particularly deep neural networks—often exhibit this characteristic. They can produce highly accurate results, yet the reasoning behind those results remains opaque. This lack of transparency is not merely a technical inconvenience; it has profound implications for accountability, fairness, and the legitimacy of decisions made by algorithmic systems.

The rise of black-box systems is closely tied to the evolution of machine learning. Traditional algorithms were designed with explicit, rule-based logic. A programmer could trace each step of the decision-making process, identify the conditions under which certain outputs were produced, and explain the rationale behind them. In contrast, many contemporary models learn patterns from data rather than following predefined rules. Their internal structure consists of layers of mathematical transformations that are optimized during training. While these transformations enable powerful predictive capabilities, they do not translate easily into human-understandable explanations.

The complexity of these models is a primary factor contributing to their opacity. Deep neural networks, for example, can contain millions or even billions of parameters. Each parameter influences the behavior of the system in subtle ways, and the interactions between parameters create a highly intricate decision landscape. Attempting to interpret such a system by examining individual components is often impractical. The model's behavior emerges from the collective interaction of its parts, making it difficult to isolate specific causes for particular outcomes.

Another contributing factor is the nature of the data used to train these systems. Machine learning models learn from patterns in data, and these patterns may be complex, high-dimensional, and non-linear. The relationships captured by the model are not always intuitive or easily expressed in simple terms. As a result, even if the internal computations are mathematically defined, their meaning in human terms may be unclear. This gap between mathematical representation and human interpretation is a key aspect of the black-box problem.

The lack of transparency has significant consequences in real-world applications. Algorithmic systems are increasingly used in domains where decisions have substantial impact, such as healthcare, finance, hiring, and criminal justice. In these contexts, understanding how a decision was made is often as important as the decision itself. For example, a patient may want to know why a particular diagnosis was recommended, or a job applicant may seek an explanation for why their application was rejected. When the system cannot provide a clear rationale, it undermines trust and raises questions about fairness and accountability.

Accountability is particularly challenging in the presence of black-box systems. In traditional decision-making processes, responsibility can often be traced to specific individuals or actions. In algorithmic systems, responsibility becomes diffuse. The outcome of a model is the result of data, design choices, and training processes, all of which may involve multiple actors. If an error or bias is identified, it may be difficult to determine who is responsible or how the issue can be corrected. This diffusion of responsibility complicates efforts to establish oversight and enforce standards.

The issue of bias is closely linked to the lack of transparency. As discussed in earlier sections, machine learning models can inherit biases from their training data. When the internal logic of the model is opaque, identifying and addressing these biases becomes more difficult. A model may produce systematically unfair outcomes without providing any clear indication of why. This makes it challenging to diagnose the source of the problem and implement corrective measures. Without transparency, bias can remain hidden, perpetuating inequities in a way that is difficult to detect and rectify.

Trust is another critical dimension affected by the black-box problem. For individuals and institutions to rely on algorithmic systems, they must have confidence in their reliability and fairness. Transparency plays a key role in building this confidence. When users can understand how a system operates and why it produces certain outcomes, they are more likely to trust it. Conversely, when decisions appear arbitrary or inexplicable, trust erodes. This is particularly important in contexts where users have limited alternatives, such as essential services or public systems.

Efforts to address the lack of transparency have given rise to the field of explainable artificial intelligence (XAI). This field focuses on developing methods to make the behavior of complex models more interpretable. Techniques such as feature importance analysis, model simplification, and visualization aim to provide insights into how models make decisions. For example, a model might indicate which variables had the greatest influence on a particular prediction, offering a partial explanation of its reasoning. While these approaches do not fully resolve the black-box problem, they represent important steps toward greater transparency.

Another approach involves the use of inherently interpretable models. These models are designed to be transparent by structure, using simpler forms of representation such as decision trees or linear models. While they may not achieve the same level of performance as more complex models in all cases, they offer the advantage of clarity. In applications where interpretability is critical, such as legal or medical decision-making, these models may be preferred despite their limitations.

Regulation and governance also play a role in addressing transparency. Some regulatory frameworks require organizations to provide explanations for algorithmic decisions, particularly when those decisions affect individuals' rights or opportunities. These requirements aim to ensure that systems are not only effective but also accountable. However, implementing such regulations can be challenging, especially when dealing with complex models that do not lend themselves easily to explanation. Balancing the need for transparency with the technical realities of modern systems is an ongoing challenge.

The trade-off between performance and transparency is a central tension in the design of algorithmic systems. Highly complex models often achieve superior performance by capturing intricate patterns in data. However, this complexity comes at the cost of interpretability. Simpler models may be easier to understand but may not perform as well in certain tasks. Designers must navigate this trade-off, considering the specific requirements and risks associated with each application. In some cases, hybrid approaches may be used, combining complex models with interpretable components to provide both accuracy and insight.

The lack of transparency also has broader societal implications. As algorithmic systems become more embedded in everyday life, their opacity can contribute to a sense of disempowerment. Individuals may feel that decisions affecting them are made by systems they do not understand and cannot influence. This can erode confidence in institutions and create a perception of arbitrariness. Ensuring that systems are transparent and accountable is therefore not only a technical issue but also a matter of public trust and democratic governance.

In addition, the concentration of expertise required to understand and manage complex models can create barriers to participation. If only a small group of specialists can interpret algorithmic systems, it limits the ability of others to engage with or challenge these systems. This concentration of knowledge can reinforce existing power dynamics, where control over technology translates into broader influence.

In conclusion, the problem of black boxes and lack of transparency is a defining challenge of the algorithmic age. It arises from the complexity of modern machine learning models, the nature of data-driven learning, and the scale at which these systems operate. While these systems offer significant capabilities, their opacity introduces risks related to accountability, bias, and trust. Addressing these challenges requires a combination of technical innovation, regulatory frameworks, and ethical consideration.

Ultimately, transparency is not an optional feature but a foundational requirement for responsible algorithmic systems. It enables understanding, supports accountability, and fosters trust. As algorithms continue to shape critical aspects of society, ensuring that their workings are accessible and interpretable becomes essential. Without transparency, the power of algorithms remains hidden, and the systems that govern modern life operate beyond the reach of meaningful scrutiny.

Chapter 4

The Psychology of Manipulation

In the evolving landscape of the algorithmic age, power is no longer exercised solely through authority, coercion, or overt control. Instead, it increasingly operates through subtle psychological mechanisms that shape perception, influence behavior, and guide decision-making. At the center of this transformation lies a critical realization: to influence what people do, one must first understand how they think. The psychology of manipulation, therefore, becomes a foundational pillar of modern algorithmic systems, bridging the gap between data, behavior, and control.

Manipulation, in its simplest form, involves influencing someone's actions or decisions, often without their full awareness. Historically, manipulation has been associated with persuasion, propaganda, or social influence—methods that rely on communication and human interaction. In the digital era, however, manipulation has become more systematic, data-driven, and scalable. It is no longer limited to individual actors or isolated campaigns; it is embedded within the architecture of platforms and technologies that millions of people interact with daily.

The key to this transformation lies in the convergence of psychology and technology. Advances in behavioral science have provided deep insights into how humans process information, make decisions, and respond to stimuli. Concepts such as cognitive biases, emotional triggers, and reward mechanisms have long been studied in psychology. What has changed is the ability to operationalize these insights through algorithms. Digital systems can now detect, model, and respond to human behavior in real time, applying psychological principles at scale and with precision.

At the heart of this process is attention. In a world saturated with information, attention becomes a scarce and valuable resource. Platforms compete to capture and retain this attention, often by leveraging psychological mechanisms that make content more engaging or compelling. Features such as notifications, personalized feeds, and infinite scrolling are not merely design choices; they are strategic implementations informed by an understanding of human behavior. They are engineered to align with how the brain responds to novelty, reward, and social validation.

The psychology of manipulation is also closely tied to the concept of habit formation. Repeated exposure to certain stimuli can create patterns of behavior that become automatic over time. Digital platforms are designed to encourage these patterns, using reinforcement techniques that reward engagement. Each interaction—liking a post, watching a video, receiving a notification—can trigger a response that reinforces the behavior, making it more likely to occur again. Over time, these interactions form habits that are deeply ingrained and difficult to disrupt.

Emotion plays a central role in this dynamic. Human decision-making is not purely rational; it is heavily influenced by emotional states. Content that evokes strong emotions—such as excitement, fear, anger, or curiosity—is more likely to capture attention and drive engagement. Algorithmic systems are designed to identify and prioritize such content, amplifying its reach. This creates an environment where emotional intensity becomes a key driver of visibility, shaping not only individual experiences but also broader patterns of information dissemination.

Another important aspect is the role of personalization. By analyzing behavioral data, systems can tailor content and experiences to individual users. This personalization creates a sense of relevance and familiarity, making interactions more engaging. However, it also narrows the range of information that users are exposed to, reinforcing existing preferences and beliefs. This can lead to the formation of echo chambers, where individuals encounter information that aligns with their views while alternative perspectives are filtered out. The result is a feedback loop that strengthens certain patterns of thought and behavior.

The subtlety of these mechanisms is what makes them particularly powerful. Unlike traditional forms of influence, which are often explicit and recognizable, algorithmic manipulation operates in the background. Users may not be aware that their experiences are being shaped or that their choices are being guided. The interface appears neutral, the content seems organic, and the experience feels personalized. Yet, beneath this surface lies a complex system of influence, continuously adapting to maximize engagement and achieve specific objectives.

This raises important questions about autonomy and agency. If decisions are influenced by systems that operate beyond conscious awareness, to what extent are those decisions truly independent? The psychology of manipulation challenges traditional notions of free will, suggesting that behavior can be shaped through subtle interventions that do not require explicit coercion. This does not mean that individuals lack agency, but it does highlight the ways in which that agency can be influenced and constrained.

The implications of this shift extend beyond individual behavior to societal dynamics. When large populations are influenced by similar mechanisms, the effects can be amplified. Public opinion, cultural trends, and social interactions can all be shaped by the underlying logic of algorithmic systems. The psychology of manipulation thus becomes a collective phenomenon, influencing not only how individuals think and act, but how societies evolve.

This chapter explores the psychological foundations of manipulation in the algorithmic age. It examines how principles of human behavior are integrated into digital systems, how these systems influence decision-making, and what this means for autonomy and control. By understanding the mechanisms at play, it becomes possible to recognize the ways in which influence operates—and to critically evaluate the systems that shape our experiences.

In a world where code interacts with cognition, the boundary between technology and psychology dissolves. The systems we use are not just tools; they are environments that shape how we think, feel, and act. To understand the algorithmic dictatorship, one must first understand the mind it seeks to influence.

Dopamine Loops and Engagement Design

In the architecture of modern digital platforms, engagement is not an incidental outcome—it is a primary objective. Systems are deliberately engineered to capture attention, sustain interaction, and encourage repeated use. At the center of this design philosophy lies a powerful neurobiological mechanism: the dopamine loop. By aligning technological features with the brain's reward system, platforms create feedback cycles that reinforce behavior, turning casual interactions into persistent habits. Understanding dopamine loops and engagement design requires examining both the underlying neuroscience and the ways in which it is operationalized within digital systems.

Dopamine is a neurotransmitter associated with motivation, reward, and learning. Contrary to common misconceptions, dopamine is not simply a "pleasure chemical." Rather, it plays a crucial role in anticipating rewards and reinforcing behaviors that lead to positive outcomes. When an individual encounters a stimulus that signals a potential reward, dopamine levels increase, creating a sense of anticipation. If the reward is realized, the behavior is reinforced; if not, the system adjusts, refining expectations for future actions. This process is fundamental to how humans learn from their environment.

Digital platforms leverage this mechanism by designing experiences that mimic reward-based learning. Each interaction—receiving a notification, seeing a new post, gaining a like or comment—serves as a potential reward. These rewards are often delivered in variable and unpredictable ways, which is a key factor in their effectiveness. Research in behavioral psychology has shown that variable reward schedules, where outcomes are uncertain, are particularly effective at reinforcing behavior. This principle is evident in activities such as gambling, where the unpredictability of outcomes drives repeated engagement. Digital platforms apply a similar logic, creating environments where users are encouraged to check, scroll, and interact in anticipation of potential rewards.

The concept of the dopamine loop emerges from this interaction between anticipation, action, and reward. A typical loop begins with a trigger—a notification, a visual cue, or a moment of idle time. This trigger prompts the user to engage with the platform. The engagement leads to a reward, such as new content or social validation, which reinforces the behavior. Over time, the user begins to associate the trigger with the reward, creating a cycle that repeats. Each iteration of the loop strengthens the association, making the behavior more automatic and habitual.

Engagement design is the process of structuring digital environments to facilitate and amplify these loops. It involves the strategic use of interface elements, content delivery mechanisms, and feedback systems to align with human psychological tendencies. One of the most prominent features of engagement design is the use of infinite scrolling. By removing natural stopping points, platforms create a continuous stream of content that encourages prolonged interaction. The absence of boundaries makes it easier for users to remain engaged, as there is always the possibility of encountering something new or rewarding.

Notifications are another critical component of engagement design. They act as external triggers that reinitiate the dopamine loop. Notifications are often designed to convey urgency or importance, prompting immediate attention. The content of notifications is carefully crafted to maximize curiosity and anticipation, encouraging users to return to the platform. Over time, users may develop a conditioned response to these triggers, checking their devices in anticipation of rewards even in the absence of notifications.

Social validation mechanisms, such as likes, comments, and shares, further reinforce engagement. These features tap into the human need for recognition and approval. Each instance of social feedback acts as a reward, reinforcing the behavior that led to it. The visibility of these metrics also introduces a comparative dimension, where users evaluate their own engagement relative to others. This can create additional motivation to participate, as users seek to maintain or enhance their social standing within the platform.

Personalization plays a significant role in optimizing dopamine loops. By analyzing user behavior, platforms can tailor content to align with individual preferences and interests. This increases the likelihood that interactions will result in rewarding experiences. Personalized feeds prioritize content that is more likely to engage the user, creating a feedback loop where preferences are continuously reinforced. While this enhances engagement, it can also narrow the range of content exposure, reinforcing existing patterns and limiting diversity.

The temporal dynamics of engagement design are also important. Timing influences how rewards are perceived and how behaviors are reinforced. Immediate rewards tend to have a stronger impact on behavior than delayed ones. Digital platforms capitalize on this by delivering rapid feedback, ensuring that actions are quickly followed by responses. This immediacy strengthens the association between behavior and reward, accelerating the formation of habits. At the same time, occasional delays or variations in reward timing can increase anticipation, further enhancing engagement.

The cumulative effect of these design elements is the creation of habitual behavior patterns. Over time, interactions with digital platforms can become automatic, integrated into daily routines. Users may find themselves engaging with platforms without conscious intention, driven by ingrained patterns of behavior. This habitual engagement is not inherently negative; it can facilitate convenience and efficiency. However, it also raises concerns about the extent to which behavior is being shaped by external systems.

One of the key challenges associated with dopamine loops and engagement design is the potential for overuse or dependency. When systems are optimized for engagement, they may encourage prolonged interaction beyond what is necessary or beneficial. The continuous availability of rewards can make it difficult for users to disengage, particularly when the experience is designed to minimize friction and maximize convenience. This can lead to patterns of use that are difficult to regulate, affecting productivity, well-being, and attention.

Another important consideration is the impact on cognitive processes. Continuous engagement with dynamic, rapidly changing content can influence attention spans and information processing. The constant stimulation provided by digital platforms may reduce the capacity for sustained focus, as users become accustomed to frequent rewards and interruptions. This shift in cognitive patterns has broader implications for learning, decision-making, and overall mental engagement.

Ethical considerations are central to the discussion of engagement design. The use of psychological principles to influence behavior raises questions about intent and responsibility. While engagement can enhance user experience, it can also be used to drive outcomes that primarily benefit the platform rather than the user. For example, maximizing time spent on a platform may increase revenue but may not align with users' long-term interests. This tension highlights the need for balance between engagement and well-being.

Designers and organizations face the challenge of aligning engagement strategies with ethical considerations. This involves evaluating not only the effectiveness of design elements but also their impact on users. Some approaches focus on promoting healthier interactions, such as introducing features that encourage breaks or provide insights into usage patterns. Others emphasize transparency, allowing users to understand how their behavior is being influenced. These efforts reflect a growing recognition of the responsibility associated with designing systems that interact with human psychology.

The broader implications of dopamine loops extend beyond individual behavior to societal dynamics. When large numbers of users are engaged through similar mechanisms, the effects can scale. Patterns of attention, communication, and interaction are shaped by the underlying design of platforms. This can influence how information spreads, how communities form, and how public discourse evolves. The design of engagement systems thus has implications not only for individual users but for collective behavior.

In conclusion, dopamine loops and engagement design represent a convergence of neuroscience, psychology, and technology. By aligning digital systems with the brain's reward mechanisms, platforms create powerful feedback cycles that reinforce behavior and sustain interaction. While these mechanisms enable engaging and personalized experiences, they also introduce challenges related to habit formation, dependency, and ethical responsibility. Understanding these dynamics is essential for navigating the algorithmic age, as it reveals how behavior is shaped at the intersection of human cognition and technological design.

Ultimately, engagement design is not merely about capturing attention—it is about shaping patterns of interaction. The systems that leverage dopamine loops do more than respond to behavior; they actively participate in its formation. Recognizing this interplay is key to understanding both the potential and the risks of modern digital environments.

Emotional Targeting and Behavioural Nudging

In the architecture of modern digital systems, influence is rarely exercised through direct commands. Instead, it operates through subtle interventions that guide behavior without overt coercion. Two of the most significant mechanisms in this process are emotional targeting and behavioral nudging. Together, they form a framework through which algorithmic systems can shape decisions, preferences, and actions by leveraging insights from psychology and behavioral science. These mechanisms do not force outcomes; they structure environments in ways that make certain choices more likely than others.

Emotional targeting is the process of identifying, analyzing, and responding to users' emotional states in order to influence behavior. Emotions play a central role in human decision-making. While rational analysis is often emphasized in traditional models of choice, research in psychology has demonstrated that emotions significantly shape how individuals perceive information, evaluate options, and act. Fear, excitement, anger, curiosity, and empathy can all affect attention and judgment. Digital systems, equipped with vast amounts of behavioral data, are increasingly capable of detecting and responding to these emotional cues.

The detection of emotional states relies on the analysis of behavioral signals. These signals may include the type of content a user engages with, the speed and pattern of interactions, and even linguistic cues in written communication. For example, the tone of language in messages or posts can provide insights into emotional states. Engagement patterns, such as repeated viewing of certain types of content, can indicate underlying moods or interests. By aggregating and analyzing these signals, systems can infer emotional tendencies with a degree of accuracy sufficient for practical application.

Once emotional states are inferred, systems can tailor content and interactions to align with or influence those states. This is where targeting occurs. Content that resonates emotionally is more likely to capture attention and drive engagement. For instance, content that evokes strong emotions—such as outrage, joy, or fear—tends to be more memorable and shareable. Algorithms can prioritize such content, increasing its visibility and impact. In this way, emotional targeting becomes a tool for amplifying engagement and guiding user behavior.

Behavioral nudging complements emotional targeting by structuring choices in a way that subtly influences decisions. The concept of nudging originates from behavioral economics and refers to the design of environments that encourage certain actions without restricting alternatives. A nudge does not eliminate choice; it alters the context in which choices are made. In digital systems, nudges are embedded in interface design, content presentation, and interaction flows.

One common example of nudging is the use of default settings. When a particular option is pre-selected, users are more likely to accept it, even if alternatives are available. This principle is widely used in digital platforms, where default configurations guide user behavior. Another example is the arrangement of options. Choices that are more prominently displayed or easier to access are more likely to be selected. By controlling the presentation of options, systems can influence decision-making without explicit persuasion.

The integration of emotional targeting and behavioral nudging creates a powerful system of influence. Emotional targeting identifies what will resonate with users, while nudging determines how that content is delivered and acted upon. For example, a platform may detect that a user is more responsive to emotionally charged content and then present such content in a way that encourages further engagement. The combination of emotional resonance and strategic presentation increases the likelihood of desired outcomes, such as prolonged interaction or specific actions.

A key feature of these mechanisms is their subtlety. Unlike traditional forms of influence, which may involve direct messaging or explicit persuasion, emotional targeting and nudging operate within the user experience itself. The interface appears neutral, and the choices remain intact. However, the structure of the environment guides behavior in ways that may not be consciously recognized. This subtlety makes these mechanisms particularly effective, as they do not trigger the same level of resistance that overt persuasion might.

The effectiveness of emotional targeting and nudging is enhanced by personalization. By analyzing individual behavior, systems can tailor interventions to specific users. This personalization increases relevance and effectiveness, as the content and nudges are aligned with individual preferences and tendencies. For example, a user who responds to social validation may be presented with features that highlight peer activity, while another user may be influenced through informational cues. This individualized approach allows systems to operate at scale while maintaining a high degree of precision.

However, the use of these mechanisms raises important ethical considerations. One of the primary concerns is the potential for manipulation. While nudging is often framed as a benign or beneficial practice, its application in digital systems can extend beyond guiding behavior toward beneficial outcomes. When nudges are designed to maximize engagement or profit, they may not align with users' best interests. For example, encouraging prolonged interaction may increase revenue for a platform but may not contribute to user well-being.

Emotional targeting also introduces risks related to exploitation. By identifying and responding to emotional states, systems can influence users at moments of vulnerability. For instance, content that exploits fear or anxiety may drive engagement but can also contribute to negative experiences. The ability to target emotions at scale amplifies these effects, potentially affecting large populations. This raises questions about the responsibility of platforms to consider the impact of their design choices on users' emotional states.

Another concern is the impact on autonomy. When decisions are influenced by subtle interventions, the extent to which those decisions are fully autonomous becomes less clear. Users may believe they are making independent choices, while in reality, their behavior is being shaped by the structure of the environment. This does not eliminate agency, but it does complicate the notion of free choice. Understanding the role of emotional targeting and nudging is therefore essential for evaluating the degree of influence exerted by digital systems.

The cumulative effects of these mechanisms can also shape broader patterns of behavior. When large numbers of users are influenced by similar systems, the impact extends beyond individual decisions to collective dynamics. For example, the amplification of emotionally charged content can influence public discourse, shaping perceptions and attitudes. Nudging mechanisms can affect how information is consumed, how decisions are made, and how interactions occur within digital environments. These effects highlight the societal implications of design choices at the platform level.

Addressing the challenges associated with emotional targeting and nudging requires a combination of technical, ethical, and regulatory approaches. Transparency is one important aspect. Providing users with information about how their data is used and how their experience is shaped can help increase awareness. However, transparency alone may not be sufficient, as the complexity of these systems can make it difficult for users to fully understand their impact.

Design practices can also be adapted to prioritize user well-being. This may involve aligning nudges with beneficial outcomes, such as encouraging healthy usage patterns or promoting diverse content exposure. Ethical guidelines can help ensure that emotional targeting is used responsibly, avoiding practices that exploit vulnerabilities or contribute to harm. In some cases, regulatory frameworks may be necessary to establish standards and accountability.

In conclusion, emotional targeting and behavioral nudging are central components of modern algorithmic systems. They enable platforms to influence behavior in subtle and scalable ways, leveraging insights from psychology and data analysis. While these mechanisms can enhance user experience and efficiency, they also introduce challenges related to manipulation, exploitation, and autonomy. Understanding how they operate is essential for navigating the algorithmic age and for developing systems that balance effectiveness with ethical responsibility.

Ultimately, these mechanisms reflect a broader shift in how influence is exercised. Rather than imposing decisions, systems shape the context in which decisions are made. In doing so, they redefine the boundaries of choice, making it increasingly important to understand not just what decisions are made, but how they are guided.

The Science of Addiction in Digital Platforms

The rapid rise of digital platforms has transformed how individuals communicate, consume information, and spend their time. Alongside these benefits, however, has emerged a growing concern: the potential for addictive patterns of use. Unlike traditional forms of addiction associated with substances, digital addiction is behavioral. It is rooted not in chemical intake, but in repeated engagement with systems designed to capture and sustain attention. The science of addiction in digital platforms lies at the intersection of neuroscience, psychology, and design, revealing how technological environments can interact with human cognitive systems to create persistent and, in some cases, compulsive behaviors.

At the core of this phenomenon is the brain's reward system. This system, primarily involving dopamine pathways, is responsible for reinforcing behaviors that are perceived as beneficial or rewarding. When an individual experiences a positive outcome—such as social approval, novelty, or achievement—the brain releases dopamine, creating a sense of satisfaction and encouraging repetition of the behavior. This mechanism is essential for learning and adaptation. However, when repeatedly activated in certain ways, it can lead to patterns that resemble addiction.

Digital platforms are uniquely positioned to engage this reward system. They provide a continuous stream of stimuli—notifications, messages, content updates, and social interactions—that can trigger dopamine release. These stimuli are often designed to be immediate, accessible, and varied, creating an environment where rewards are frequent and unpredictable. The unpredictability is particularly important. Research in behavioral psychology has shown that variable reward schedules—where rewards occur at irregular intervals—are more effective at reinforcing behavior than consistent rewards. This principle, long observed in contexts such as gambling, is embedded in many digital experiences.

For example, social media platforms present users with feeds that are constantly refreshed with new content. Each interaction—scrolling, clicking, or tapping—carries the possibility of encountering something rewarding. The user does not know in advance which action will produce a satisfying outcome, creating a sense of anticipation. This anticipation itself can be rewarding, encouraging continued engagement. Over time, the act of checking the platform becomes habitual, driven by the expectation of potential rewards.

Notifications play a significant role in this process. They act as external triggers that initiate engagement. A notification signals the possibility of a reward—someone has liked a post, sent a message, or interacted with content. The uncertainty of what the notification contains enhances its impact. Users are prompted to check their devices, often immediately, reinforcing the connection between the trigger and the reward. Repeated exposure to this cycle can lead to conditioned responses, where the mere presence of a notification—or even the expectation of one—elicits engagement.

Another important factor is social validation. Human beings are inherently social, and the need for recognition and approval is deeply embedded in psychological processes. Digital platforms amplify this dynamic by quantifying social interactions through metrics such as likes, comments, shares, and follower counts. These metrics provide immediate feedback, acting as rewards that reinforce behavior. Each instance of social validation can trigger dopamine release, encouraging users to seek similar outcomes in the future. The visibility of these metrics also introduces a comparative element, where users evaluate their standing relative to others, further motivating engagement.

The design of digital platforms often incorporates features that minimize friction and maximize accessibility. Infinite scrolling, autoplay videos, and seamless navigation reduce the effort required to continue interacting with the platform. By removing natural stopping points, these features encourage prolonged use. The absence of clear boundaries makes it easier for users to lose track of time, as there is always more content available. This continuous flow aligns with the brain's tendency to seek ongoing stimulation, reinforcing engagement patterns.

Habit formation is a key component of digital addiction. Habits are behaviors that become automatic through repetition. In the context of digital platforms, repeated engagement with reward-based systems can lead to the development of habits that are triggered by specific cues. For example, a user may habitually check their phone when experiencing boredom, waiting in line, or waking up in the morning. These behaviors become ingrained, often occurring without conscious intention. The transition from intentional use to habitual engagement is a critical step in the development of addictive patterns.

The concept of reinforcement learning provides a framework for understanding this process. In reinforcement learning, behaviors are shaped by rewards and penalties. Positive reinforcement increases the likelihood of a behavior being repeated, while negative outcomes decrease it. Digital platforms primarily rely on positive reinforcement, providing rewards that encourage continued use. The variability and immediacy of these rewards enhance their effectiveness, making the learning process more rapid and robust.

However, not all aspects of digital addiction are purely positive reinforcement. In some cases, negative emotions can also drive engagement. Feelings such as anxiety, loneliness, or fear of missing out (FOMO) can motivate users to interact with platforms in search of relief or connection. This creates a cycle where engagement is used as a coping mechanism, which in turn reinforces the behavior. The platform becomes both the source of stimulation and a perceived solution to emotional discomfort.

The impact of these mechanisms extends beyond individual behavior to cognitive processes. Continuous exposure to rapid, varied stimuli can affect attention and information processing. Users may become accustomed to short bursts of content, reducing their capacity for sustained focus. The constant availability of digital engagement can also influence decision-making, as individuals may prioritize immediate rewards over long-term considerations. These changes in cognitive patterns highlight the broader implications of digital addiction.

It is important to note that not all engagement with digital platforms constitutes addiction. The distinction lies in the degree of control and the impact on well-being. Healthy use involves intentional interaction that aligns with individual goals and needs. Addictive patterns, by contrast, are characterized by a loss of control, where users engage in behaviors despite negative consequences. These consequences may include reduced productivity, disrupted sleep, or diminished social interaction in offline contexts.

The ethical implications of designing for engagement are significant. Platforms are often incentivized to maximize user interaction, as engagement is closely linked to revenue models such as advertising. This creates a tension between business objectives and user well-being. Designing systems that prioritize engagement without considering their impact can contribute to the development of addictive patterns. Addressing this issue requires a balance between creating engaging experiences and ensuring that those experiences do not undermine user autonomy or health.

Efforts to mitigate digital addiction include both design interventions and user awareness. Some platforms have introduced features that provide insights into usage patterns, allowing users to monitor their behavior. Others have implemented tools that encourage breaks or limit notifications. From a design perspective, introducing friction or natural stopping points can help users regulate their engagement. However, the effectiveness of these measures depends on their integration into the broader system and the willingness of users to adopt them.

Education and awareness also play a role in addressing digital addiction. Understanding the mechanisms that drive engagement can empower users to make more informed choices about their interactions. Recognizing the role of dopamine loops, variable rewards, and habit formation can help individuals identify patterns and adjust their behavior. However, awareness alone may not be sufficient, as the design of platforms continues to evolve and adapt.

In conclusion, the science of addiction in digital platforms is rooted in the interaction between human neurobiology and technological design. By leveraging the brain's reward system, platforms create environments that encourage repeated engagement and, in some cases, habitual or compulsive use. While these mechanisms can enhance user experience, they also introduce challenges related to control, well-being, and ethical responsibility.

Ultimately, digital addiction is not solely a function of individual behavior; it is shaped by the systems within which that behavior occurs. Understanding these systems is essential for developing approaches that balance engagement with well-being. As digital platforms continue to play a central role in daily life, addressing the science of addiction becomes increasingly important for ensuring that technology serves, rather than dominates, human experience.

Attention as the New Commodity

In the architecture of the digital economy, attention has emerged as one of the most valuable and contested resources. Unlike traditional commodities—such as land, labor, or capital—attention is intangible, finite, and deeply tied to human cognition. It represents the capacity to focus, process information, and engage with stimuli. In an environment saturated with information, where content is abundant and continuously expanding, attention becomes scarce. This scarcity transforms attention into a commodity—something that can be captured, measured, traded, and monetized.

The concept of attention as a commodity is rooted in the imbalance between information supply and human capacity. While digital systems can generate and distribute vast amounts of content at negligible cost, the human ability to consume and process that content remains limited. Each individual has a finite amount of time and cognitive energy, and this limitation creates competition. Platforms, advertisers, and content creators all compete for slices of this limited resource. The result is an attention economy, where success is determined not by the quantity of content produced, but by the ability to capture and retain attention.

In this economy, attention is both the input and the output of value creation. Platforms provide content and services designed to attract users, and in return, users provide their attention. This attention is then monetized, often through advertising or data-driven services. The more attention a platform can capture, the more opportunities it has to generate revenue. This creates a feedback loop in which platforms are incentivized to maximize engagement, continuously refining their strategies to hold users' focus for longer periods.

The commodification of attention is closely linked to the design of digital systems. Platforms are engineered to optimize for engagement, using a combination of algorithms, interface design, and behavioral insights. Features such as personalized feeds, notifications, and autoplay are designed to capture attention and reduce friction in user interaction. These features are not incidental; they are strategic elements that align with the economic objective of maximizing time spent on the platform.

Measurement is a key component of attention as a commodity. Unlike traditional resources, attention must be quantified through proxies. Metrics such as time spent, click-through rates, engagement levels, and retention rates are used to assess how effectively attention is captured and maintained. These metrics provide feedback to platforms, guiding the optimization of content and design. They also serve as the basis for transactions in the attention economy. Advertisers, for example, pay for access to user attention, often measured in impressions or interactions.

The role of algorithms in managing attention is central. Algorithms determine what content is presented to users, in what order, and with what emphasis. By analyzing behavioral data, these systems can predict which content is most likely to capture attention and prioritize it accordingly. This creates a curated experience, where the flow of information is shaped by the objective of maximizing engagement. The algorithm becomes a gatekeeper, filtering and organizing content in ways that align with the platform's goals.

Personalization enhances the efficiency of attention capture. By tailoring content to individual preferences, platforms increase the likelihood that users will find the content relevant and engaging. This personalization is driven by data, which provides insights into user behavior and interests. While personalization can improve user experience, it also narrows the range of content exposure, reinforcing existing preferences and creating feedback loops. Users are more likely to encounter content that aligns with their past behavior, which in turn shapes future behavior.

The competition for attention has significant implications for content creation. In an environment where attention is scarce, content must compete not only on quality but on its ability to capture interest quickly.

This often leads to the prioritization of content that is emotionally engaging, visually striking, or immediately rewarding. Headlines, thumbnails, and opening sequences are designed to attract attention within seconds. This emphasis on immediacy can influence the nature of content itself, favoring formats that are optimized for quick consumption over those that require sustained focus.

The commodification of attention also affects how information is valued. In traditional contexts, information might be evaluated based on accuracy, depth, or relevance. In the attention economy, visibility becomes a key determinant of value. Content that captures attention is amplified, while content that does not may remain unseen, regardless of its quality. This dynamic can shape public discourse, as topics that generate high engagement receive more visibility, influencing what is discussed and how it is perceived.

Another important aspect is the temporal dimension of attention. Attention is not only limited in quantity but also in duration. Platforms seek not just to capture attention, but to sustain it over time. This leads to the design of experiences that encourage prolonged engagement, such as continuous content streams or episodic formats. The goal is to extend the duration of attention, increasing the total amount of time users spend interacting with the platform.

The economic value of attention has led to the emergence of new business models. Advertising remains a primary mechanism, where attention is sold to advertisers seeking to reach specific audiences. However, other models have also developed, including subscription services and data-driven products. In each case, attention plays a central role, either as a direct source of revenue or as a means of generating data that can be monetized.

The implications of attention as a commodity extend beyond economics to cognitive and social dimensions. Continuous competition for attention can affect how individuals process information and allocate their focus. The constant availability of stimuli may lead to fragmented attention, where focus is divided across multiple sources. This can impact cognitive processes such as memory, comprehension, and decision-making. The ability to sustain attention on complex tasks may be challenged by the prevalence of short, engaging content.

From a social perspective, the attention economy influences how individuals interact and communicate. Social interactions are often mediated through platforms that prioritize engagement, shaping how messages are conveyed and received. The visibility of content can affect social dynamics, as individuals seek to capture attention within their networks. This can influence behavior, encouraging actions that are more likely to generate engagement.

Ethical considerations are central to the discussion of attention as a commodity. The design of systems that compete for attention raises questions about responsibility and impact. While capturing attention is essential for the functioning of digital platforms, excessive or manipulative practices can have negative consequences. For example, strategies that exploit cognitive biases or emotional triggers may increase engagement but may not align with users' well-being. Balancing the objectives of engagement and user welfare is a key challenge in the design of digital systems.

Regulation and awareness are potential responses to these challenges. Policies that address transparency, data use, and platform practices can help ensure that attention is managed responsibly. At the same time, increasing user awareness about how attention is captured and monetized can empower individuals to make more informed choices. Understanding the mechanisms of the attention economy is a step toward navigating its effects.

In conclusion, attention as the new commodity reflects a fundamental shift in the structure of the digital economy. It transforms human focus into a resource that can be captured, measured, and monetized. This transformation is driven by the abundance of information and the scarcity of cognitive capacity, creating a competitive environment where attention is highly valued. While this system enables new forms of interaction and innovation, it also introduces challenges related to cognition, behavior, and ethics.

Ultimately, the commodification of attention highlights the interplay between human cognition and technological systems. It reveals how value is created not just through what is produced, but through what is perceived and engaged with. In the algorithmic age, attention is not merely a byproduct of interaction—it is the foundation upon which digital systems are built and sustained.

Chapter 5

social media as a Control System

Social media platforms are often presented as tools for communication, connection, and expression—digital spaces where individuals share ideas, build relationships, and participate in global conversations. While these functions are real, they represent only one layer of a much deeper and more complex system. Beneath the surface of posts, likes, and interactions lies an infrastructure designed not just to connect people, but to organize, prioritize, and influence human behavior at scale. In this sense, social media can be understood not merely as a communication tool, but as a control system.

A control system, in its broadest definition, is a mechanism that regulates behavior within a system to achieve specific outcomes. It operates by collecting input, processing that input, and generating outputs that influence future behavior. Social media platforms fit this model with remarkable precision. They collect vast amounts of behavioral data from users, process that data through algorithmic systems, and deliver curated content that shapes how users interact, think, and respond. The result is a continuous feedback loop in which user behavior is both the input and the product of the system.

At the center of this process are algorithms that determine what content is seen, when it is seen, and how it is presented. Unlike traditional media, where content distribution is relatively static, social media feeds are dynamic and personalized. Each user experiences a unique stream of information, tailored to their preferences, behaviors, and engagement patterns. This personalization enhances relevance and engagement, but it also introduces a layer of control. By deciding which content is prioritized and which is suppressed, the system shapes the user's perception of reality.

This curation is not neutral. It is guided by specific objectives, often centered around maximizing engagement and retention. Content that captures attention—whether through emotional intensity, novelty, or social relevance—is more likely to be promoted. Over time, this creates an environment where certain types of content are amplified, while others remain less visible. The user's experience is shaped not by the totality of available information, but by a filtered subset that aligns with the system's goals.

The feedback loop inherent in social media systems reinforces this dynamic. As users interact with content, they generate data that informs future recommendations. If a user engages with a particular type of content, the system is more likely to present similar content in the future. This creates a self-reinforcing cycle, where preferences are continuously refined and reinforced. While this can enhance user satisfaction, it can also narrow the range of perspectives encountered, leading to the formation of echo chambers and filter bubbles.

Beyond content curation, social media platforms influence behavior through their design. Features such as notifications, likes, shares, and comments are not merely functional; they are mechanisms that encourage interaction and shape user behavior. These features are informed by psychological principles, designed to trigger responses and sustain engagement. The system does not simply respond to user behavior—it actively shapes it, guiding how users interact with content and with each other.

The concept of social validation plays a significant role in this process. Metrics such as likes and shares provide immediate feedback, reinforcing certain behaviors and discouraging others. Users may adjust their actions based on the feedback they receive, seeking to maximize positive responses. This creates a form of behavioral conditioning, where the system indirectly influences how users present themselves and what content they produce.

The implications of social media as a control system extend beyond individual behavior to collective dynamics. When millions of users interact within the same system, the effects of algorithmic control can scale. Trends, narratives, and public opinion can be shaped by the way content is distributed and amplified. The system becomes a mediator of information flow, influencing not only what individuals see, but what becomes visible at a societal level.

This raises important questions about power and responsibility. Social media platforms, by virtue of their control over information distribution, hold significant influence over public discourse. Decisions about algorithm design, content moderation, and platform policies can have far-reaching effects. Yet, these decisions are often made within private organizations, guided by internal objectives rather than public accountability. This creates a tension between the role of social media as a public space and its operation as a private system.

Another critical aspect is the invisibility of control. Unlike traditional systems of authority, where control is explicit and recognizable, the influence exerted by social media is often subtle and embedded within the user experience. Users may not be aware of how their interactions are being shaped or how their perceptions are being influenced. The system operates in the background, continuously adjusting and optimizing, making control less visible but no less effective.

The framing of social media as a control system does not imply that users are passive or powerless. Individuals retain agency and the ability to make choices. However, it highlights the context in which those choices are made—a context that is structured and influenced by algorithmic systems. Understanding this context is essential for evaluating the role of social media in modern society.

This chapter examines social media through the lens of control systems, exploring how data, algorithms, and design interact to shape behavior and information flow. It seeks to uncover the mechanisms that underlie everyday interactions and to analyze their broader implications. By doing so, it provides a framework for understanding social media not just as a platform for communication, but as a system that organizes and influences the digital experience.

In a world where information is abundant and attention is limited, the ability to control what is seen and how it is experienced becomes a powerful form of influence. Social media platforms, through their architecture and operation, have become central actors in this dynamic. To understand their impact, one must look beyond their surface functions and examine the systems that drive them.

Algorithmic Feeds and Content Prioritization

In the modern digital ecosystem, the way information is presented is as important as the information itself. Social media platforms and content-driven applications no longer rely on chronological timelines or neutral distribution systems. Instead, they employ algorithmic feeds—dynamic systems that select, rank, and prioritize content based on a combination of data, behavioral patterns, and predefined objectives. These feeds act as intermediaries between users and information, shaping not only what is seen but also how it is perceived. Understanding algorithmic feeds and content prioritization is essential to grasp how digital platforms influence attention, behavior, and ultimately, reality itself.

At its core, an algorithmic feed is a system designed to filter and organize content for individual users. Unlike static systems where all content is equally accessible, algorithmic feeds curate a personalized stream of information. This personalization is driven by data—specifically, data about user behavior, preferences, and interactions. Every action a user takes, from liking a post to pausing on a video, contributes to a profile that informs future content selection. The feed is continuously updated, adapting in real time to reflect the user's evolving patterns.

Content prioritization is the mechanism through which this selection occurs. Given the vast volume of content available, platforms must decide which pieces of information are presented and in what order. This decision is not random; it is guided by ranking algorithms that assign scores to content based on various factors. These factors may include relevance, engagement potential, recency, and user relationships. The content with the highest scores is placed at the top of the feed, where it is most likely to be seen and interacted with.

Engagement is often a central metric in this process. Platforms are designed to maximize user interaction, as engagement is closely tied to revenue models such as advertising. Content that generates high levels of engagement—likes, comments, shares, or viewing time—is more likely to be prioritized. This creates a feedback loop where engaging content is amplified, increasing its visibility and reach. Over time, this dynamic can influence the types of content that are produced, as creators adapt to the preferences of the algorithm to maximize exposure.

Personalization enhances the effectiveness of content prioritization. By tailoring feeds to individual users, platforms increase the likelihood that the content presented will resonate. This is achieved through machine learning models that analyze patterns in user behavior. For example, if a user frequently engages with a particular type of content, the system will prioritize similar content in the future. This creates a sense of relevance and familiarity, making the feed more engaging. However, it also narrows the range of content exposure, reinforcing existing preferences and limiting diversity.

The concept of relevance in algorithmic feeds is not purely objective. It is defined by the system's objectives and the data it uses. What is considered relevant is often what is most likely to engage the user, rather than what is most accurate or informative. This distinction is critical, as it highlights the difference between content that is prioritized for engagement and content that is prioritized for value. The alignment of relevance with engagement can lead to the amplification of content that is emotionally charged or sensational, as such content tends to attract more interaction.

Temporal factors also play a role in content prioritization. While many platforms have moved away from strictly chronological feeds, recency remains an important variable. Newer content is often given a temporary boost, allowing it to gain initial visibility. This creates a dynamic environment where content is continuously refreshed, encouraging users to return frequently to stay updated. The interplay between recency and engagement ensures that both new and popular content can be surfaced, maintaining a balance between novelty and familiarity.

Another important aspect of algorithmic feeds is the role of network effects. Content from users with larger or more active networks is more likely to be prioritized, as it has a higher potential for engagement. This can create disparities in visibility, where certain voices are amplified while others remain less prominent. The structure of the network itself influences content distribution, as connections and interactions shape the flow of information. This introduces a social dimension to content prioritization, where relationships and influence play a role alongside algorithmic factors.

The design of algorithmic feeds also incorporates elements of experimentation and optimization. Platforms continuously test different configurations, adjusting parameters to improve performance metrics. This process, often referred to as A/B testing, allows systems to identify which approaches yield higher engagement. The feed is not static; it evolves based on data-driven insights, refining its behavior over time. This adaptability enhances efficiency but also adds complexity, as the system's behavior may change in ways that are not immediately visible to users.

The implications of algorithmic feeds extend beyond individual user experience to broader societal dynamics. By shaping what information is visible, these systems influence how users perceive events, trends, and issues. The prioritization of certain types of content can affect public discourse, highlighting some topics while downplaying others. This can create a perception of reality that is filtered through the lens of the algorithm, rather than reflecting the full spectrum of available information.

One of the most discussed consequences of algorithmic feeds is the formation of echo chambers. When users are repeatedly exposed to content that aligns with their existing preferences and beliefs, they may encounter fewer opposing perspectives. This can reinforce viewpoints and reduce exposure to diverse information. The personalization that enhances engagement can also contribute to fragmentation, where different users experience distinct versions of the same platform, each shaped by their individual data profiles.

Filter bubbles are closely related to this phenomenon. They occur when algorithms selectively present information based on user behavior, effectively isolating users from content that falls outside their established patterns. While filter bubbles can increase relevance, they also limit the breadth of information exposure. This can have implications for critical thinking and informed decision-making, as users may not encounter a balanced range of perspectives.

Transparency is a significant challenge in the context of algorithmic feeds. The criteria used to prioritize content are often not fully disclosed, making it difficult for users to understand why certain content appears in their feed. This lack of visibility can create a sense of opacity, where the system's behavior is not easily interpretable. Efforts to increase transparency, such as providing explanations for content recommendations, aim to address this issue, but achieving full clarity remains complex.

Ethical considerations are central to the design and operation of algorithmic feeds. The prioritization of engagement can conflict with other values, such as accuracy, fairness, and well-being. For example, content that is highly engaging may not always be reliable or beneficial. Balancing these considerations requires careful design choices and, in some cases, external regulation. The responsibility of platforms extends beyond optimizing metrics to considering the broader impact of their systems.

From a technical perspective, content prioritization involves multiple layers of computation. Data is collected and processed to generate features, which are then used by ranking models to score content. These models may incorporate various signals, including user behavior, content attributes, and contextual factors. The output is a ranked list of content, which is presented to the user through the interface. Each step in this process contributes to the final experience, highlighting the complexity of the system.

In conclusion, algorithmic feeds and content prioritization are central to the functioning of modern digital platforms. They determine how information is organized, presented, and consumed, shaping user experiences and influencing behavior. While these systems enhance personalization and engagement, they also introduce challenges related to diversity, transparency, and societal impact. Understanding their mechanisms is essential for navigating the algorithmic age and for evaluating the role of digital platforms in shaping information ecosystems.

Ultimately, algorithmic feeds are not neutral conduits of information—they are active systems that structure the flow of content. By prioritizing certain information over others, they influence what is seen, what is ignored, and how reality is constructed in the digital space.

Echo Chambers and Filter Bubbles

In the contemporary digital environment, the flow of information is no longer neutral or uniformly distributed. Instead, it is shaped by algorithmic systems that curate content based on user behavior, preferences, and interactions. Within this framework, two closely related phenomena have emerged as defining features of the modern information ecosystem: echo chambers and filter bubbles. Both concepts describe environments in which individuals are exposed primarily to information that aligns with their existing beliefs and perspectives. While they share similarities, they arise through different mechanisms and have distinct implications for how people perceive and engage with the world.

An echo chamber refers to a social environment where ideas, opinions, and beliefs are amplified and reinforced through repeated exposure within a closed network. In such environments, individuals interact primarily with others who share similar viewpoints. This repetition creates a feedback loop, where the same ideas are echoed back, gaining perceived validity through frequency and consensus. The social dimension of echo chambers is critical; they are not solely the result of algorithms but also of human tendencies to seek out and associate with like-minded individuals.

Filter bubbles, on the other hand, are primarily driven by algorithmic personalization. They occur when digital systems selectively present information based on a user's past behavior, effectively filtering out content that does not align with established patterns. Unlike echo chambers, which are shaped by social interactions, filter bubbles are the product of automated processes. Algorithms analyze user data to predict preferences and prioritize content accordingly. Over time, this personalization narrows the range of information exposure, creating a bubble in which users encounter a limited subset of perspectives.

The emergence of these phenomena is closely tied to the design and objectives of digital platforms. As discussed in previous sections, platforms are optimized for engagement. Content that resonates with users is more likely to capture attention and generate interaction.

Algorithms learn from user behavior, identifying patterns that indicate preference. If a user frequently engages with a particular type of content or viewpoint, the system interprets this as a signal of interest and increases the likelihood of presenting similar content in the future. This creates a self-reinforcing cycle, where preferences are continuously reinforced and alternative perspectives are less likely to appear.

Human psychology plays a significant role in this process. Individuals have a natural tendency toward confirmation bias—the inclination to seek out information that confirms existing beliefs while avoiding information that challenges them. This bias influences how users interact with content, as they are more likely to engage with material that aligns with their views. Algorithms, in turn, interpret this engagement as a preference, further amplifying similar content. The interaction between human bias and algorithmic design creates a powerful feedback loop that reinforces echo chambers and filter bubbles.

The structure of social networks also contributes to the formation of echo chambers. Digital platforms often connect users based on shared interests, relationships, or interactions. Over time, these networks can become homogeneous, as individuals are more likely to form connections with others who share similar perspectives. Within these networks, information circulates in a way that reinforces group consensus. Dissenting views may be less visible or actively discouraged, further strengthening the echo chamber effect.

The consequences of echo chambers and filter bubbles extend beyond individual experience to collective dynamics. One of the most significant impacts is the polarization of opinions. When individuals are consistently exposed to one-sided information, their views may become more extreme. The absence of contrasting perspectives reduces opportunities for critical evaluation and dialogue. As a result, differences between groups can become more pronounced, leading to divisions that are difficult to bridge.

Another important consequence is the distortion of perceived reality. In a filter bubble, the information presented to a user is not a comprehensive representation of available content but a curated subset. This can create a skewed perception of what is common, important, or true. For example, if a user's feed consistently highlights certain topics or viewpoints, they may perceive these as more prevalent than they actually are. This distortion can influence decision-making, as individuals base their judgments on incomplete or biased information.

The amplification of misinformation is another critical concern. Echo chambers and filter bubbles can facilitate the spread of inaccurate or misleading information. When false information aligns with the beliefs of a particular group, it may be more readily accepted and shared. The lack of exposure to corrective information allows such content to persist and gain traction. Algorithms that prioritize engagement may inadvertently amplify misinformation if it generates strong reactions, further complicating efforts to ensure information accuracy.

The role of algorithms in these dynamics raises questions about responsibility and design. While personalization enhances user experience by making content more relevant, it also contributes to the narrowing of information exposure. Designers must consider how to balance personalization with diversity, ensuring that users are exposed to a range of perspectives. Some approaches involve introducing mechanisms that promote content diversity or provide users with greater control over their feeds. However, implementing these solutions is complex, as they may conflict with engagement objectives.

Transparency is another important aspect of addressing echo chambers and filter bubbles. Users often have limited awareness of how their content is curated. Providing insights into how algorithms operate and why certain content is shown can help users understand the dynamics of their information environment. This awareness can encourage more deliberate engagement, as users recognize the influence of personalization on their experience.

Education and critical thinking are also essential in navigating these phenomena. Understanding the role of confirmation bias and the mechanics of algorithmic curation can help individuals evaluate information more effectively. By actively seeking diverse perspectives and questioning assumptions, users can mitigate the effects of echo chambers and filter bubbles. However, this requires effort and awareness, as the default experience of many platforms is designed to reinforce existing patterns.

From a broader perspective, echo chambers and filter bubbles highlight the interplay between technology and society. They are not solely the result of algorithmic design or human behavior, but a combination of both. Addressing their impact requires a holistic approach that considers technical, social, and cognitive factors. This includes rethinking platform design, promoting media literacy, and fostering environments that encourage open dialogue.

It is also important to recognize that not all aspects of these phenomena are negative. Personalization can enhance relevance and efficiency, allowing users to access content that aligns with their interests. Echo chambers can provide a sense of community and shared identity. The challenge lies in balancing these benefits with the need for diversity and critical engagement. Ensuring that users have access to a broad range of information while maintaining relevance is a key objective in the design of digital systems.

In conclusion, echo chambers and filter bubbles are central features of the modern information ecosystem. They arise from the interaction between human psychology, social networks, and algorithmic systems. While they enhance personalization and engagement, they also introduce challenges related to polarization, misinformation, and perception. Understanding these dynamics is essential for navigating the algorithmic age and for developing systems that support informed and balanced engagement.

Ultimately, the existence of echo chambers and filter bubbles underscores the importance of how information is curated and consumed. In a world where algorithms mediate access to knowledge, the structure of information environments becomes a critical factor in shaping individual and collective understanding.

Viral Mechanics and Emotional Amplification

In the digital ecosystem, information does not spread randomly. The rapid dissemination of content—commonly described as "going viral"—is the result of identifiable mechanisms that govern how information moves across networks. These mechanisms are not purely organic; they are shaped by a combination of human psychology, social dynamics, and algorithmic design. At the center of this process lies emotional amplification, a phenomenon in which content that evokes strong emotional responses is more likely to be shared, engaged with, and propagated. Understanding viral mechanics and emotional amplification reveals how digital systems prioritize certain types of content and how these priorities influence collective behavior.

Viral mechanics refer to the structural and behavioral processes that enable content to spread rapidly through a network. These processes involve multiple stages: exposure, engagement, sharing, and reinforcement. For content to become viral, it must first be visible to users. This visibility is often determined by algorithmic systems that prioritize content based on engagement potential. Once exposed, the content must capture attention and prompt interaction. Engagement signals—such as likes, comments, and shares—indicate to the system that the content is valuable, increasing its likelihood of being shown to additional users. This creates a cascading effect, where each layer of engagement expands the content's reach.

The network structure of social media platforms plays a crucial role in this process. Users are connected through relationships, forming clusters and communities. When content is shared within these networks, it can quickly reach a large number of individuals, particularly if it resonates with multiple groups. The presence of highly connected users—often referred to as influencers or hubs—can accelerate this process. When such users engage with content, their large audiences amplify its visibility, increasing the likelihood of further dissemination.

Emotional amplification is a key driver of viral mechanics. Human beings are more likely to engage with and share content that evokes strong emotions. Emotions such as joy, surprise, anger, fear, and outrage can increase the perceived importance of information, prompting users to react and share. This is not merely a behavioral tendency; it is rooted in cognitive processes. Emotional stimuli are processed more rapidly and remembered more vividly than neutral information. As a result, emotionally charged content is more likely to capture attention and persist in memory.

Algorithms are designed to detect and prioritize content that generates high engagement, and emotional content often meets this criterion. When users interact with emotionally charged material, the system interprets this as a signal of relevance and amplifies its distribution. This creates a feedback loop in which emotional content is more likely to be promoted, leading to increased exposure and further engagement. Over time, this dynamic can shape the overall content landscape, favoring material that elicits strong reactions.

The nature of emotional amplification can vary depending on the type of emotion involved. Positive emotions, such as amusement or inspiration, can drive sharing by creating a sense of connection and enjoyment. Negative emotions, particularly those associated with high arousal—such as anger or fear—can be even more potent. These emotions often trigger a sense of urgency or importance, motivating users to share information quickly. Content that combines emotional intensity with perceived relevance is particularly likely to spread, as it aligns with both psychological and social drivers of engagement.

The design of digital platforms enhances these dynamics. Features such as share buttons, reaction metrics, and comment sections facilitate rapid interaction. The ease of sharing reduces the effort required to propagate content, enabling users to act on emotional impulses with minimal friction. At the same time, visible engagement metrics provide social proof, signaling to users that content is popular or significant. This can influence behavior, as individuals are more likely to engage with content that others have already interacted with.

Temporal factors also influence viral mechanics. The speed at which content spreads is often critical. Rapid initial engagement can trigger algorithmic amplification, as the system detects a surge in activity and increases distribution. This creates a window of opportunity where content can achieve widespread visibility. Conversely, content that fails to gain traction early may remain limited in reach, regardless of its intrinsic value. Timing, therefore, plays a crucial role in determining whether content becomes viral.

Another important aspect is the role of narrative and format. Content that is easily understood, visually engaging, or structured as a compelling story is more likely to capture attention and be shared. Simplicity and clarity facilitate quick processing, making it easier for users to engage and pass the content along. Visual elements, such as images and videos, can enhance emotional impact, increasing the likelihood of engagement. The combination of narrative structure and emotional resonance creates a powerful mechanism for dissemination.

The implications of viral mechanics and emotional amplification extend beyond individual content to broader information ecosystems. The prioritization of emotionally engaging material can influence what topics gain visibility and how they are framed. Issues that evoke strong reactions may dominate attention, while more nuanced or complex topics receive less exposure. This can shape public discourse, as the most visible content is not necessarily the most accurate or informative, but the most engaging.

The amplification of emotional content also has implications for misinformation. False or misleading information can spread rapidly if it aligns with emotional triggers. The combination of emotional resonance and algorithmic amplification can allow such content to reach large audiences before it can be corrected. This highlights the challenges of managing information quality in environments optimized for engagement.

From a behavioral perspective, repeated exposure to emotionally amplified content can influence perception and attitudes. When users encounter similar types of content consistently, it can reinforce certain viewpoints and shape beliefs. This effect is compounded by the feedback loops inherent in algorithmic systems, where engagement with specific content leads to increased exposure to similar material. Over time, this can contribute to the formation of polarized perspectives and reinforce existing biases.

Addressing the challenges associated with viral mechanics and emotional amplification requires a multifaceted approach. Platform design can play a role in moderating the spread of content, for example by introducing friction in sharing processes or adjusting ranking algorithms to consider factors beyond engagement. Transparency in how content is prioritized can help users understand the dynamics of their information environment. Additionally, promoting media literacy and critical thinking can empower individuals to evaluate content more effectively.

Ethical considerations are central to this discussion. While emotional engagement is a natural and valuable aspect of human interaction, its exploitation for the purpose of maximizing attention raises questions about responsibility. Platforms must balance the objectives of engagement and user well-being, ensuring that the amplification of content does not lead to harm or distortion. This involves not only technical adjustments but also broader considerations of how digital systems interact with human psychology.

In conclusion, viral mechanics and emotional amplification are fundamental components of the modern digital ecosystem. They explain how content spreads, why certain information gains prominence, and how user behavior is influenced. These processes are driven by the interaction of psychological tendencies, social networks, and algorithmic systems. While they enable rapid communication and engagement, they also introduce challenges related to information quality, perception, and societal impact.

Ultimately, the dynamics of virality are not accidental; they are structured and reinforced by the systems that govern digital platforms. Recognizing these dynamics is essential for understanding how information flows in the algorithmic age and for developing approaches that support balanced and informed engagement.

The Illusion of Free Choice

In the modern digital environment, individuals are presented with an unprecedented range of options. From the content they consume to the products they purchase, the choices appear vast, personalized, and readily accessible. This abundance creates the perception of autonomy—the belief that decisions are freely made, guided solely by individual preferences and intentions. However, beneath this surface lies a more complex reality. The choices individuals encounter are often structured, filtered, and influenced by algorithmic systems. This creates what can be described as the illusion of free choice: a condition in which individuals feel autonomous while their options and decisions are subtly shaped by external mechanisms.

At its core, the illusion of free choice arises from the distinction between the existence of options and the structure of those options. While users may technically have access to a wide range of possibilities, the way these possibilities are presented influences how decisions are made. Digital platforms rarely display all available options equally. Instead, they prioritize certain content, products, or actions based on algorithmic criteria. This prioritization determines what is visible, what is prominent, and what is likely to be chosen. In this context, choice is not eliminated, but it is guided.

The process begins with data. As users interact with digital systems, they generate behavioral data that reflects their preferences, habits, and tendencies. This data is analyzed to create profiles that inform future recommendations. Algorithms use these profiles to predict what users are likely to engage with and adjust the presentation of options accordingly. For example, a user who frequently watches a particular genre of content will be presented with similar options in the future. While this personalization enhances relevance, it also narrows the range of choices that are actively presented.

This narrowing effect is not immediately apparent to users. The interface remains open, and alternative options are often technically available. However, the prominence of certain choices over others creates a bias in decision-making. Users are more likely to select options that are easily accessible, prominently displayed, or repeatedly presented. This phenomenon is well-documented in behavioral science, where the framing and positioning of choices significantly influence outcomes. In digital systems, this principle is operationalized through design and algorithms.

The role of defaults is particularly significant in shaping perceived choice. Default options are pre-selected or presented as the standard choice, requiring no additional effort from the user. Research has shown that individuals are more likely to accept default settings, even when alternatives are available. Digital platforms leverage this tendency by configuring defaults in ways that align with their objectives. Whether it is privacy settings, subscription options, or content recommendations, defaults can guide behavior without restricting alternatives. The user retains the ability to change the setting, but the effort required to do so creates a barrier that reinforces the default choice.

Another mechanism contributing to the illusion of free choice is the sequencing of options. The order in which choices are presented affects how they are perceived and evaluated. Options that appear first or are highlighted are more likely to be selected. Algorithmic systems use ranking models to determine this order, prioritizing options based on predicted engagement or relevance. This creates a structured decision environment where certain choices are more visible and accessible than others. The user experiences a range of options, but the structure of that range influences the outcome.

Emotional and psychological factors further complicate the notion of free choice. As discussed in earlier sections, digital systems are designed to engage users by leveraging cognitive biases and emotional triggers. These factors influence decision-making in ways that may not be consciously recognized. For example, content that evokes strong emotions is more likely to capture attention and influence choices. Similarly, social validation mechanisms—such as likes and reviews—can affect how options are perceived. When a choice is associated with positive feedback from others, it may appear more desirable, guiding the user toward that option.

The feedback loop inherent in algorithmic systems reinforces these dynamics. Each decision a user makes provides data that informs future recommendations. Over time, this creates a cycle where preferences are continuously refined and reinforced. The system becomes increasingly accurate in predicting behavior, and the user's experience becomes more aligned with past actions. While this enhances personalization, it also limits exposure to new or diverse options. The user's choices are shaped by a history of interactions, creating a path-dependent experience.

The illusion of free choice is not limited to individual decisions; it extends to broader patterns of behavior. When large numbers of users interact with similar systems, the cumulative effect can shape trends, preferences, and cultural norms. The choices that are most visible and accessible become more widely adopted, influencing collective behavior. This dynamic highlights the role of algorithmic systems in shaping not only individual experiences but also societal patterns.

One of the key challenges in understanding the illusion of free choice is its subtlety. Unlike overt forms of control, where options are explicitly restricted, algorithmic influence operates within the framework of choice. Users are not forced to make specific decisions; they are guided toward certain outcomes through the structure of the environment. This makes the influence less visible and more difficult to recognize. The perception of autonomy remains intact, even as the decision-making process is shaped by external factors.

The implications of this phenomenon are significant. Autonomy is a fundamental aspect of human agency, and the ability to make independent decisions is central to individual and societal functioning. When choices are influenced in ways that are not fully transparent, it raises questions about the extent of that autonomy. This does not imply that individuals lack agency, but it does suggest that agency operates within a context that is structured and influenced by algorithmic systems.

Ethical considerations are central to this discussion. The design of systems that influence choice must balance effectiveness with respect for user autonomy. While guiding users toward relevant or beneficial options can enhance experience, it can also lead to manipulation if not carefully managed. Transparency, user control, and accountability are important factors in addressing these concerns. Providing users with insights into how their choices are shaped and offering mechanisms to adjust preferences can help mitigate the effects of structured decision environments.

Another important aspect is the role of awareness. Understanding how digital systems influence choice can empower users to engage more critically with their options. Recognizing the impact of defaults, ranking, and personalization can help individuals make more deliberate decisions. However, this requires a level of digital literacy that may not be uniformly distributed across populations. Efforts to increase awareness and education are therefore essential in addressing the broader implications of algorithmic influence.

In conclusion, the illusion of free choice reflects a fundamental tension in the digital age. While individuals are presented with a wide array of options, the structure and presentation of those options are shaped by algorithmic systems. This creates an environment where choices are guided rather than fully independent. The interplay between data, design, and psychology influences decision-making in ways that are often subtle and difficult to detect.

Ultimately, the concept of free choice in digital systems must be understood within the context of these influences. Autonomy is not eliminated, but it is mediated by the systems through which choices are presented. Recognizing this mediation is essential for navigating the algorithmic landscape and for ensuring that the design of digital systems supports, rather than undermines, meaningful choice.

Conclusion

Rewriting the Code of Civilization

The journey through the algorithmic age reveals a profound transformation in how power operates, how decisions are made, and how human behavior is shaped. What began as a series of technological advancements—algorithms, data systems, machine learning—has evolved into an infrastructure that influences nearly every aspect of modern life. From the information we consume to the choices we make, from the systems that govern economies to those that shape social interaction, code has become a central force in the organization of civilization. To understand this shift is to recognize that we are not merely using technology—we are living within systems that continuously interpret, predict, and influence us.

The concept of an algorithmic dictatorship does not imply a single controlling authority, but rather a distributed network of systems that collectively shape outcomes. These systems operate through data extraction, predictive modeling, and behavioral influence, often without explicit visibility. They do not command; they guide. They do not impose; they optimize. Yet, their cumulative effect can be as powerful as any traditional form of control. By structuring the flow of information and the environment of choice, they redefine the boundaries within which human agency operates.

Rewriting the code of civilization, therefore, is not about rejecting technology, but about rethinking its role and design. It requires a shift from passive adoption to active engagement—a recognition that the systems we build reflect the values we prioritize. Algorithms are not inherently neutral; they embody decisions about what to measure, what to optimize, and what to prioritize. As such, the future of these systems depends on the principles that guide their development.

One of the most critical steps in this process is awareness. Understanding how algorithmic systems function—how they collect data, how they influence behavior, and how they shape outcomes—is essential for navigating their impact. Awareness transforms users from passive participants into informed actors, capable of questioning and evaluating the systems they interact with. It provides the foundation for critical engagement, enabling individuals to recognize patterns of influence and make more deliberate choices.

However, awareness alone is not sufficient. Structural changes are necessary to address the broader implications of algorithmic systems. This includes rethinking data governance, ensuring that individuals have greater control over their information and how it is used. Ownership and consent must be redefined in ways that reflect the realities of the digital age, moving beyond procedural agreements toward meaningful participation. Transparency must be enhanced, allowing users to understand how decisions are made and to hold systems accountable.

Ethical design is another cornerstone of this transformation. The objectives embedded within algorithms must align with broader societal values, balancing efficiency and engagement with fairness and well-being. This requires a deliberate effort to consider the impact of design choices, not only in terms of performance but also in terms of their effect on individuals and communities. Incorporating principles such as fairness, inclusivity, and accountability into system design can help ensure that technology serves collective interests rather than narrow objectives.

Regulation and governance play a crucial role in shaping the future of algorithmic systems. As these systems become more integrated into critical aspects of society, the need for oversight increases. Policies that address issues such as data privacy, algorithmic transparency, and market concentration can help establish boundaries and standards. However, regulation must be adaptive, capable of evolving alongside technological advancements. It must also strike a balance between enabling innovation and protecting public interests.

At the same time, responsibility is not confined to institutions and organizations. Individuals also play a role in shaping the digital environment. Choices about how to engage with technology, what content to consume, how to interact with platforms, and how to manage attention—contribute to the broader dynamics of the system. Collective behavior influences algorithmic outcomes, creating a reciprocal relationship between users and systems. By engaging more consciously, individuals can influence the direction of these systems over time.

The future of civilization in the algorithmic age is not predetermined. It is shaped by the interplay of technology, policy, and human behavior. While the current trajectory highlights challenges related to control, bias, and autonomy, it also presents opportunities. The same systems that enable influence can be designed to support empowerment. Data can be used to enhance understanding rather than exploit behavior. Algorithms can be structured to promote diversity and balance rather than reinforce narrow patterns.

Rewriting the code of civilization, therefore, is an ongoing process. It involves questioning assumptions, redefining objectives, and continuously evaluating the impact of technological systems. It requires collaboration across disciplines—technologists, policymakers, ethicists, and users—each contributing to a more balanced and equitable digital ecosystem. This process is not about eliminating complexity, but about managing it in ways that align with human values.

Ultimately, the algorithmic age challenges us to reconsider what it means to live in a world shaped by code. It invites us to move beyond viewing technology as a neutral tool and to recognize it as a system of influence that must be understood, guided, and, when necessary, redefined. The question is not whether algorithms will shape the future—they already do. The question is how we choose to shape them in return.

In this sense, rewriting the code of civilization is both a responsibility and an opportunity. It is a call to ensure that the systems we build reflect not only our capabilities, but our aspirations—for autonomy, fairness, and a future where technology enhances, rather than constrains, human experience.

www.ingramcontent.com/pod-product-compliance
Lightning Source LLC
Chambersburg PA
CBHW041300210926
51847CB00009B/90
9789699797781